SOFT-SOAPING INDIA

THE WORLD OF INDIAN
TELEVISED SOAP OPERAS

SOFT-SOAPING INDIA
THE WORLD OF INDIAN TELEVISED SOAP OPERAS

K. Moti Gokulsing

Trentham Books

Stoke on Trent, UK and Sterling, USA

Trentham Books Limited

Westview House   22883 Quicksilver Drive
734 London Road   Sterling
Oakhill   VA 20166-2012
Stoke on Trent   USA
Staffordshire
England ST4 5NP

First published 2004

British Library Cataloguing-in-Publication Data
A catalogue record for this book is available from the
British Library

ISBN 1 85856 321 6

Designed and typeset by Trentham Print Design Ltd., Chester
and printed in Great Britain by Cromwell Press Ltd., Wiltshire.

Acknowledgements
Cover images and slogan: This is not the only place you'll find
bold, determined and gritty women like yourself.
By kind permission of Zee Network (UK).

Map on page xi: from Pamela Shurmer-Smith,
India Globalization and Change published by Arnold,
a member of the Hodder Headline Group (2000)
ISBN 0340 70578 7 (pb)
(Reprinted by permission of Hodder Arnold)

With thanks to Population Communications International
(PCI) for their kind permission to reproduce material from
their report.

Contents

Dedication
To Seetah (1932 – 2002)
In loving memory

'*Un seul être vous manque, et tout est dépeuplé*'
Alphonse de Lamartine L'Isolement

Acknowledgements

This book has had a difficult gestation period. Early in 1999, my late wife and I started watching soap operas on ZeeTV. Unable to find relevant reading materials about them in England, I commissioned Mr B S Chandrasekhar, then Director of Audience Research Unit at *Prasar Bharati* (Broadcasting Corporation of India), to carry out a small scale survey about the role and impact on Indian audiences in Delhi and Mumbai of two popular soap operas on ZeeTV – *Amanat* and *Aashirwaad*. Mr Chandrasekhar and his team carried out the survey and started sending me data in 2000. However, my wife fell seriously ill during that time and the project had to be shelved.

In the course of the three years during which this study was undertaken on an on/off basis, I have incurred debts of gratitude to a considerable number of people, too many to mention individually. The following, however, deserve special mention.

Mr B S Chandrasekhar not only conducted the survey, he also provided me with relevant reading materials. He sent me his report in a publishable format, authorising me to use the materials as much as I wish. Without his help, this study would not have seen the light of day.

Professor Arvind Singhal has helped considerably with advice, guidance about sources and constructive feedback. I am greatly indebted to him for sharing his expertise on the Entertainment-Education Communication Strategy and on *Hum Log* with me.

Dr Jim McKenzie read parts of the manuscript in its early days and helped with the statistical data. Dr Cornel DaCosta made some very useful comments and suggestions and Professor Wimal Dissanayake provided intellectual and moral support. I am grateful to them for their friendship over the years.

Mr John M Antonio James, Executive Associate of Population Communication International for permission to use materials from their report on *Humraahi*.

Pat Silverlock who word processed parts of the draft and Sunny Lochab who helped me cope with the frequent glitches of the computer.

Kevin Rego, Corporate Communications Manager at Asia TV Limited, who provided me with ZeeTV materials.

Gillian Klein for her editorial expertise and professional touch which have really transformed the messy draft I gave her and sharpened its focus.

My daughters, Shishana and Nishani and my son-in-law, David for their much needed support and encouragement.

Although the help, support and advice of all the people mentioned above are gratefully acknowledged, I, the author, take full responsibility for any shortcomings that remain.

Glossary

This glossary, compiled from a variety of sources, is highly selective, but it contains much of the basic terminology used in this book.

Adharma – Practices and beliefs deemed to be contrary to the prescribed ethical or religious code.

Audience Segmentation – Fine-tuning messages to fit a relatively homogeneous segment in order to maximise communication effects.

Avatar – incarnation, usually of the god Vishnu.

Babri Masjid – Mosque built in the sixteenth century in Ayodhya in northern India. It was destroyed by Hindutva crowds on 6 December, 1992.

Backward Classes – Members of the Scheduled Castes and the other low-ranking groups (sometimes referred to as Other Backward Classes – OBCs)

Behaviourally Oriented Parasocial Interaction – the degree to which individuals talk with other audience members or with the media characters.

Bharat – the land of India.

Bharatiya Janata Party (BJP) – Formed in 1980 out of the remains of the Jan Sangh political party. The BJP is a Hindu nationalist political party and represented the first unified party in opposition to the Congress Party. Is currently the leading party in the government.

Brahmin – a member of the priestly caste, the highest caste.

Cognitively Oriented Parasocial Interaction – the degree to which audience members pay careful attention to characters of a media programme and think about its educational content after viewing it.

Crore – a unit of measure equal to 10 million rupees (or 100 lakh).

Dacoit – robber, criminal

Dalit – Literally 'oppressed' – Sanskrit word meaning split, broken but now refers to 'untouchables' (Harijans – Children of god in Mahatma Gandhi's phrase).

Darshan – means seeing and being seen by the deity.

Desh – Country.

Dharma – has a variety of meanings – may mean religion, duty, law, morality, a divinely ordained code of proper conduct

Dowry – gifts transferred by the bride's family to the bride or bridegroom on the occasion of marriage.

Entertainment-education – the process of purely designing and implementing a media message to both entertain and educate in order to increase knowledge about an issue, create favourable attitudes, and change overt behaviour.

Extended family – group comprising two or more families of procreation united lineally and/or collaterally.

Formative evaluation – a type of research conducted while an activity, process, or system is being developed or is ongoing to improve effectiveness.

Ghara/Ghar/Gara – household, home.

Hindu rashtra – the Hindu nation or state.

Hindutva – literally 'Hindu-ness' (Hindu cultural identity) a political ideology of Hindu nationalism propounded by V.D. Savarkar in 1923. The key slogan used by the Hindu right wing.

Karma – one's actions, duty. Related to the idea of heaven and hell as well as rebirth.

Mandir – a temple.

Manusmriti – Law of Manu – a religio-legal text describing duties of different social groups.

Media advocacy – the strategic use of the mass media for advancing social or public policy initiatives.

Meta-communication – communication about communication e.g. epilogues.

Murti – an icon of a deity.

Myths – legendary stories that express the beliefs of a people, often serving to explain natural phenomena or the origins of a people.

Panchayat – institution of local government/ a local council.

Parasocial interaction – the seemingly face-to-face interpersonal relationships that develop between a viewer and a popular media personality like a television performer.

Prosocial behaviours – are those that are desirable and beneficial to other individuals or to society at large.

Puja – worship in which offerings are made to a deity.

Ramjanmabhoomi – a political movement to build a temple in honour of Lord Ram at the site of Babri Masjid in Ayodhya (the alleged site of Ram's birth).

Sangh Parivar – 'the family of RSS, VHP and BJP – created and influenced organisations'.

Sadhu – Hindu holy man.

Sati – widow sacrifice/widow immolation – the practice of wife / widow burning.

Self-efficacy – an individual's perception of his or her capability to deal effectively with a situation, and one's sense of perceived control over a situation.

Summative evaluation – research that is conducted in order to form a judgement about the effectiveness of the communication intervention in reaching its objectives.

Abbreviations

AIDMK   All India Anna Dravida Munnetra Kazagham (Tamil political party)

AIR   All India Radio

BJP   Bharatiya Janata Party (national political party)

CNN   Cable News Network

DART   Doordarshan Audience Research Television (ratings system)

DD   Doordarshan (state TV in India)

DMK   Dravida Munnetra Kazagham (Tamil political party)

IMRB   Indian Market Research Bureau

MARG   Indian Market Research Organisation

MTV   Music TV (part of Viacom)

NASA   National Aeronautics and Space Administration (USA)

NCAER   National Council of Applied Economic Research

NDTV   New Delhi Television

NGO   Non-Governmental Organisation

NRS   National Readership Survey

OBC   Other Backward Classes

RSS   Rashtriya Swayamsevak Sangh (right wing Hindu organisation)

SC   Scheduled Caste

SITE   Satellite Instructional Television Educational Project

ST   Scheduled Tribe

STAR   Satellite Television Asia Region

TRP   Television Rating Point

UNESCO   United Nations Educational, Scientific and Cultural Organisation

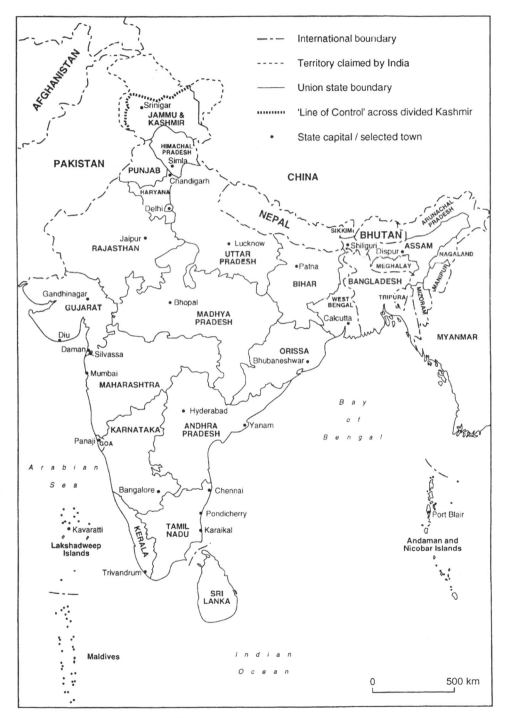

From Pamela Shurmer-Smith, *India Globalization and Change.*

Introduction

If Asia must no longer be thought of as Other, this is not just because of the moral/ideological liability of the discourse of Orientalism, but because the region that has come to be called Asia has become an inherent part, and force in, the contemporary global condition. (Ang and Stratton, 1996:20)

At any time across the dateline, millions of people are watching Indian soap operas on television. Integral to Indian popular culture today, they are telecast on Indian, cable and satellite channels all over the world. They are watched in affluent western apartments and in communal settings in remote villages and teeming cities on every continent.

The uniqueness of Indian soap operas reflects the uniqueness of India. They use a combination of conventional and non-conventional designs, thereby producing a unique textual form. Yet, whereas the literature on conventionally designed soap operas such as *Coronation Street, Neighbours, Dallas, EastEnders* is extensive, comparative little research has been carried out on Indian soap operas either for themselves or in the wider context of a new India where the search for national unity, territorial integrity and the ideology of consumerism have become dominant. Some aspects of the uniqueness of India are outlined in this introduction, to provide a context for an understanding of its soap operas.

At the beginning of the twenty first century, India is different from the country that became independent over half a century ago. It is the largest democracy in the world. With a billion people, India will, by 2040, be the most populous country in the world, if present demographic trends hold (*Times of India*, 19 January 1997). India is also the world's most complex nation-people are of numerous cultural and ethnic backgrounds, speaking fifteen main languages and hundreds of dialects. Indeed, India is pluralist and diverse in a way that few countries are, as Sen has observed:

> It is not easy to think of another country that has as many flourishing languages and literatures. What is central to our present turmoil is, of course, religious diversity, and there again our position is fairly unique. The vast

majority of Indians may be Hindus, but we have more than a hundred million Muslims (India has the third largest Muslim population in the world), we have more Sikhs than any other country, more Jains too, more Parsees as well; India has had Christians for over fifteen hundred years (much longer than Britain has had any) and while the number of Indian Buddhists today may be small, ours is the birthplace of Buddhism. I don't believe there exists another country the religious diversity of which begins to match ours. (1993:39-40)

In recent years, however, the fabric of Indian society has been increasingly severely tested. Despite the decline of the Congress Party and the problems of governability, the assassination of two former Prime Ministers, the continuing terrorism in the state of Kashmir, the rise of Hindu nationalism and the aggravation of communal violence, India has not so far disintegrated as a society. This is not to ignore issues such as social cleavages within India and the fragile relationship between Hindus and Muslims that have surfaced more recently. Indeed, at the time of independence, India appeared as a country unlikely to sustain democratic institutions. That it did was due largely to the four Nehruvian principles – socialism, secularism, democracy and non-alignment – which, as Vanaik (2001:43) states, 'officially guided India's modernizing project since 1947'. In a greatly changed India a closer look at these Nehruvian principles helps us understand Indian soap operas, since these principles are reflected in them in one form or another.

Of the four Nehruvian principles, democracy is so far the least compromised. It formally began in 1950 when India as a Republic drew upon Western concepts of democracy. Thus, its Preamble has a familiar sound:

It is the responsibility of the Republic to ensure that all citizens enjoy JUSTICE, social, economic and political; LIBERTY of thought, expression, belief, faith and worship; EQUALITY of status and opportunity; and ... FRATERNITY assuring the dignity of the individual and the unity of the nation. (Norton, 2001:41)

As Norton (2001:43) observes 'democracy in a parliamentary form of government, as implemented in 1950 by the Constitution of the Republic of India, has worked well'. It is through its democratic institutions and especially through the ballot box that India has been able to weather the recent traumatic political changes – the erosion of the Congress Party as the single party rule at the national level accelerated by Indira Gandhi's declarations of the state of emergency (1975-1977) to protect herself from a legal challenge to her office, the destruction of the Babri Mosque on 6 December 1992, the rise of Hindu nationalism and the dramatic rise to political prominence of the *Bharatiya Janata Party* (BJP). India's democracy, examined in a volume edited by Atul Kohli (2001), however, masks some dismal failures.

Widespread poverty (vividly described by Naipaul (1992) on his visit to the Bombay slum called Dharavi), the persistence of foul hygienic conditions, the lack of basic amenities in many parts of India, language diversity often resulting in barriers to communication, the increasing communal conflicts affecting not only the relationship between Hindus and Muslims but also Christians so that there are many Indias within India. Norton asserts that

> One basic problem is that democracy in India has been implemented in political structures – a constitution and a parliament – that are not indigenous to India, but were instead imposed from the West. (2001:43)

As a result, not only is the notion of India as a nation problematic but so is nationalism. The forging of a national identity became a major factor for the BJP since Congress' version of secularism had failed to bind a nation in the making.

It was precisely to rebuild the nation that Hindu nationalists took advantage of the failure of the Congress party in the 1980s to replace it as the centre of the political system. The destruction of the Babri mosque in 1992 and, in particular the way in which it was carried out with the then leader of the BJP, L. K. Advani, touring the country on a '*Rath Yatra*' (chariot tour), reminding Hindus of the horse-drawn carts of *The Mahabharata*, turned the unthinkable into a historical fact (Vanaik, 2001).

The question of who actually is a Hindu received some sort of answer from Savarkar, father of Hindu nationalism. According to him, a Hindu means a person who regards

> the land...from the Indus to the Seas as his fatherland as well as his Holyland. The definition is territorial (land between the Indus and the Seas), genealogical ('fatherland'), and religious ('holyland'). Hindus, Sikhs, Jains and Buddhists can be part of this definition, for they meet all three criteria. All these religions were born in India. Christians, Jews, Parsis and Muslims, however, can meet only two criteria. India is not their 'holyland'. (quoted in Varshney, 1993:231)

Of the three themes about India – territorial, cultural and religious – the last one means that

> India is originally the land of the Hindus, and it is the only land which Hindus can call their own... Most of India is, and has been, Hindu by religion ... A great deal of ethnic diversity may exist within Hindu society: a faith in Hinduism brings the diversity together. India viewed in this fashion is a Hindu nation. (Varshney, 1993:235)

To what extent the telecasting of the sacred epics of *The Ramayana* and *The Mahabharata* on Doordarshan in the 1980s helped the cause of the Hindu nationalists is discussed in Chapter 3.

The BJP and its associates have redefined the notion of secularism, the second Nehruvian principle. Writers such as Madan (1987) and Nandy (1988) have argued secularism is unsuited to India and must inevitably come to grief (Varshney, 1993:228). Varshney (1993) further argues that there are different varieties of secularism and that the kind practised by Indira Gandhi and Rajiv Gandhi was not a logical culmination of the secularism of Nehru.

Vanaik (2001:56) goes further, saying that the secularism practised by the Congress Party – of the Gandhian tradition – meant 'religious tolerance' – 'itself portrayed as the enduring spirit of India's ancient – i.e. Hindu – civilization'. Drawing attention to the caste system as viciously intolerant, Vanaik states that the 'religious tolerance' version of secularism is 'historically false and strategically disastrous'. The Hindu Right have been able to whip up religious fervour because the politics of impartial involvement – all round appeasement – was unsuited to the political and economic circumstances of the 1980s.

Economically, India is expected by the year 2020 to be the fourth largest economy in the world in terms of purchasing power. The ground for this dramatic u-turn was laid partly by the minority Congress government of Narasimha Rao in the early 1990s with its liberalisation and globalisation policies. Socialism (the third Nehruvian principle) in India took a back seat when India's links with the Soviet industrial model and Soviet patronage severed owing to the Soviet Union 'dying without notice'; the government of Rao introduced substantial fiscal, industrial and agricultural policies and achieved significant results before it lost out in the 1996 elections (Gupta, 1998). Economic progress has been to some extent driven by the governments' constant five-year plans. The first five year plan ran from 1951-1956 and each one followed the last without a break, so that the ninth ended in 2002.

Nevertheless, now that India is part of a globalised world, it is playing a major role in the international markets for goods, services and technology. Its software industry has now reached nearly five billion US dollars – its software exports have grown more than twenty times in the last seven years. Major players include Unilever, IBM, Nestlé, PepsiCo, Procter and Gamble, General Electric. The impact of globalisation on India's economy is profound.

Running parallel to the impact of globalisation on the economy of India is the impact of satellite television on the lifestyle of its inhabitants. This is equally re-markable for while radio and cinema reached India soon after their establishment in the West, television broadcasting started in September 1959, more than two decades after it began in the Western world. And as Page and Crawley have documented, the rapid spread of satellite television in recent years has made a huge impact on the choice of viewing available to audiences in South Asia, not just in the cities but increasingly in town and rural areas as well (2001:blurb).

A striking example of the influence of globalisation in India is provided by Johnson

> Just hours after my arrival in Mumbai International Airport, I rode in a taxi on my way to Pune. As we crossed over the long toll bridge leading out of the city I observed a man on an elephant on the side of the road. The man looked as if he was a *Sadhu* because he had long hair and a beard and was dressed in only a loincloth. As we drove up next to him I could see that he had three ash lines on his forehead which confirmed that he was on a religious journey. As we got closer I noticed something that I will never forget. This man, who typified the romantic view of traditional India, was wearing a walkman. And what appeared to be the elephant rocking him back and forth was actually him moving to the sounds of the music in his head set... (2000:147)

Music, and film music in particular, is the major ingredient of popular culture in India. But in recent years, soap operas have become the most popular genre on Indian and Satellite Channels. The designs of Indian soap operas are a mix of conventional and non-conventional elements. These provide an interesting mixture of influences, producing a unique textual form on Indian television. Chapter 1 of this book examines this mix of designs, describing and comparing conventional and entertainment-education soap operas. Chapter 2 charts the origins and development of Doordarshan, the Indian State television, and the arrival of cable and satellite channels in the late 1980s/early 1990s, in particular Zee TV. They have been instrumental in creating a new South Asia popular culture (Page and Crawley 2001: blurb). In Chapter 3 a number of soap operas telecast on Doordarshan are analysed along religious, political, social, sociological, cultural and economic variables. Chapter 4 focuses on soap operas on satellite channels, mainly on Zee TV and particularly on two successful soap operas – *Amanat* (Sacred trust) and *Aashirwaad* (Blessing), which are taken as case studies. Chapter 5 examines theoretical and methodological issues relevant to the study of soap operas in general and televised Indian soap operas in particular. In Chapter 6 family relationships, birth control and women-oriented soap operas are explored.

Chapter 7 focuses on televised Indian soap operas in relation to the ideology of consumption. Chapter 8, the conclusion, looks at issues of national integration, identity and citizenship in India and at entertainment on satellite channels in a globalised India. The bibliography provides guidance to readers who may wish to pursue further aspects of this little known, but highly fascinating dimension, of Indian popular culture.

Given the general lack of standardisation in translations of Indian languages into English, as Rajadhyaksha and Willemen (1994) note in their *Encyclopaedia of Indian Cinema*, I have not tried to standardise the spelling of names and titles of soap operas. For example, the forms Ramjanmabhoomi/ Ram Janmabhumi; Manusmriti/Manusmrti; Ghara/Ghar; Humraahi/Hum Raahi; Rajani/Rajni; Choudhry/Chaudhari; Bhagavadgita/Bhagavad Gita are used interchangeably. Aashirwaad is spelt differently – Aashirvad – in some writings.

CHAPTER 1

What is an Indian soap opera?

Much has been written about the general features of the soap opera as a genre. Soaps are a form of serialised dramatic television broadcast (Cantor and Pingree, 1983:19).

Their origins are usually traced to the radio soaps in the USA in the early twentieth century, as Allen (1985) has argued in his ground-breaking study. Given the pejorative use of the term opera and the strong criticisms of popular culture as a field of study voiced by a number of writers (Leavis and Thompson, 1933; Ortega Gasset, 1932; Adorno, 1991), it is interesting to note that

> Yoking together 'Soap' and 'Opera' marks their distance between the opera's own thematic preoccupations (legend, myth, royalty) and presumed audience (the educated elite) and those of the radio serial: as the 1939 Newsweek article defines it, the soap opera brings 'the hardworking housewife the Real Life adventures of Real People'. (Allen, 1985:9)

The serialisation of novels dates back to the 1850s when most of the works of Charles Dickens, for example, were read as magazine serials. In much of the literature on televised drama series, the terms series and serials are often used interchangeably but it is important to draw a distinction between series and serials.

> While series feature the same characters regularly, each individual programme has its own discrete storyline, generally resolved by the end of the programme. Serials, by contrast, may have stories resolved within one episode but have at least one storyline that continues from episode to episode... Soap Opera (by contrast) is an indefinite serial that in theory can continue forever. Commonly Soap Operas feature multiple and interlocking narratives, some of which may be short lived, while others go on for months or even years. Ultimate closure is indefinitely postponed – in this sense Soap Opera is open-ended as opposed to the characteristic closed narrative form of situation comedy. (Goodwin and Whannel, 1990:18)

It is possible to overstate the difference between series and serials, since a number of productions such as, for example, Casualty in the UK 'completed narratives in

1

each episode are often combined with much longer running narratives which not only continue from one episode to the next, but sometimes even from one season to the next' (O'Donnell, 1999:2).

However, as far as Indian soap operas are concerned, there is some debate about their label. One ingredient of soap operas – regular and frequent transmission particularly in daytime – was not typical of Indian soap operas telecast on Indian and satellite channels. Manohar Shyam Joshi, the scriptwriter of such soap operas as *Hum Log* (We People), *Buniyaad* (Foundation), *Humraahi* (Co-Travellers), is reported to have said:

> Well, strictly speaking none of these – Hum Log, Buniyaad and Humraahi – could claim to have the well-defined parameters of a soap opera in the Western sense of the term. For none of these was a 'daytime, five-times-a-week telecast, nor was it so planned structurally. (Saksena, 1996:115)

But there is some confusion here. Before the 1980s soap operas were telecast only between 9am and 3pm. These soap operas were slow moving and tended to emphasise the emotional. However, since the 1980s

> Soap operas have moved into the evening time slots – a space previously reserved for crime dramas and films. Prime-time soap operas usually have much more action. (Stewart *et al*, 2001:286)

On a more substantive point, Mitra (1993:85-86) takes issue with Singhal and Rogers (1987), who assert that pro-development soap operas in India and other developing nations are quite different from televised soap operas in the United States. Mitra's (1993) view is that structurally Indian soap operas share many similarities with those in the USA. For example, both kinds of soap operas have what Allen (1985) describes 'as a paradigmatic structure consisting of a large number of characters and a syntagmatic structure where the narrative never ends but a major narrative question is left unanswered at the end of each episode'. Consequently, Mitra suggests that, as far as Indian soap operas are concerned, one just needs to qualify them by attaching such labels as pro-development, religious or social 'to further qualify these programmes' (Mitra, 1993:86).

Although Indian soap operas undoubtedly share some characteristics with those of the USA, those based on the *Sabido* technique (see page 3 for an explanation) are different in their design, content and the target audience. For in practice typically the televised soap opera will have most or all of the following features

- It has a loosely knit story line or rather more like a collection of stories with a number of competing and complementary sub plots

- It is aimed predominantly at female viewers, hence it focuses on female characters, the politics of family relationships, particularly large families

- It has usually a large and constant cast
- It involves cheap production costs
- It uses the cliff hanger to ensure continued viewing
- It appeals to advertisers. (See e.g.Livingstone, 1990)

Conventionally designed Indian soap operas have many of the features listed above and so are similar to those of the USA. A common thread of all soap operas is how fiction is encoding real life. As Oltean put it

> ...paradoxically enough, these fictions offer fewer obstacles to interpretation than stories about non-fictitious events and actors...What is interesting too is not the constative (demonstrative or factual) mode but rather the performative mode, and the coherence and the credibility of the telling rather than the accuracy of this depiction of reality. (1993:8)

Another important feature of all soap operas is their popularity. Throughout the world televised soap operas enjoy very high audience ratings. For instance, in Britain *Coronation Street* and *EastEnders* have been in the top five rated shows for many years. What, then, accounts for their universal popularity?

As far back as 1944, Herzog identified three primary reasons:

- Audience members look forward to the emotional release they receive through the storylines and characters. They laugh, cry, and want to be surprised by a dramatic turn of events

- Soap operas provide the audience members with an opportunity for fantasy fulfilment (wishful thinking). Many audience members report that while their own lives are sad and tedious, they can abandon them for a short while through the lives of the fictional characters

- Audience members often seek information and advice from their favourite characters. (quoted in Singhal and Rogers,1999:59)

While the vast majority of soap operas are conventionally designed, Indian soap operas combine both conventional as well as non-conventional designs as stated earlier on. Conventionally designed soap operas are primarily entertaining and only incidentally educational. A number of Indian soap operas follow this pattern, but others, particularly those on Doordarshan, (*doordarshan* means distant vision) the Indian State television, deliberately combine entertainment with education and use the model of entertainment-education communication strategy first developed by Miguel Sabido of Mexico in order to bring about social change.

Entertainment-Education Communication Strategy

Much has been written in recent years about the Sabido technique (for example, Brown, 1990; Nariman, 1993; Singhal, Obregon and Rogers, 1994; Singhal and

Obregon, 1999 among others). Originally, the entertainment-education strategy in television was discovered more or less by accident in Peru in 1969 when the television soap opera *Simplemente Maria* was broadcast (Singhal and Rogers, 1999: 14). This was the most popular *telenovela* (television novel or soap opera) of all time in Latin America.

Inspired by the overwhelming success of *Simplemente Maria*, Miguel Sabido, a television-writer-producer in Mexico and leader of the Mexican Institute of Communication Studies, developed a theory-based production method for the social use of commercial soap operas. Between 1975 and 1982 Sabido produced

> seven entertainment-education television Soap Operas for Television... Sabido's work in Mexico directly inspired various other entertainment-education efforts worldwide' including India (Singhal and Obregon, 1999:68).

But what are the theoretical components of Sabido's communication strategy? Drawing on a conversation which Singhal and Obregon (1999:68) had with Miguel Sabido and on the comprehensive account of the Entertainment-Education Communication Strategy given by Brown, Singhal and Rogers (1988) and Singhal and Rogers (1999:60), a comparison between conventional soap operas and entertainment-education soap operas yields the following Venn diagram:

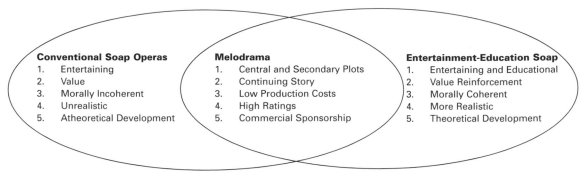

Conventional Soap Operas
1. Entertaining
2. Value
3. Morally Incoherent
4. Unrealistic
5. Atheoretical Development

Melodrama
1. Central and Secondary Plots
2. Continuing Story
3. Low Production Costs
4. High Ratings
5. Commercial Sponsorship

Entertainment-Education Soap
1. Entertaining and Educational
2. Value Reinforcement
3. Morally Coherent
4. More Realistic
5. Theoretical Development

(Source Brown, Singhal and Rogers, 1988)

Clearly, the Entertainment-Education Communication Strategy differs from the conventional soap opera technique in the following ways:

• Conventional soap operas are not purposely educational and any learning stemming from the content of the soap operas is incidental (*Dallas, Dynasty, East-Enders*).

• Conventional soap operas are designed primarily to attract audiences and their components generally consist of sex, violence, greed and materialism—undesirable values which 'sell' (example *Dallas*). Entertainment education is designed to promote and reinforce particular prosocial beliefs and values. 'It is the process of embedding educational content within entertainment messages in order to increase individuals' knowledge about an educational issue, create favorable attitudes, and change overt behaviour concerning the educational issue' (Singhal and Rogers 1999:413) (e.g. gender equality in *Hum Log*).

• Conventional soap operas are often morally incoherent; no clear distinctions are made between good and bad behaviours (binary oppositions). Entertainment-Education Soap Operas seek to avoid sending confusing signals to their audience. In some Entertainment-Education Soap Operas, 'a carefully constructed epilogue, delivered by a respected authority figure, reinforces these moral distinctions for audience individuals' (example Ashok Kumar in *Hum Log*; he is obviously not part of the soap opera).

• Conventional soap operas are usually unrealistic fantasies because they depict inaccurate portrayals of life as experienced by most of their viewers. In contrast, Entertainment-Education Soap Operas are designed to fit the reality of the target audience conditions. Formative evaluation is conducted to assess the needs of the target audience – in the case of *Hum Log*, for example, the family planning theme telecast in the first thirteen episodes was alienating the audience – consequently the soap opera was ushered back to the drawing board. Instead, the rest of the soap opera – 143 episodes – generally focused on the broader theme of the status of women in Indian society.

Finally, probably the most important difference between conventional soap operas and entertainment-education soap operas is that the latter are theory-based whereas the former are generally atheoretical. The theories which guided Sabido's entertainment-education communication strategy include the following:

* Albert Bandura's Social Learning theory (1977, 1986, 1997) (in 1986 Bandura used the term social cognitive theory in his new book)

* Eric Bentley's dramatic theory (1967)

* Carl Jung's theory of the collective unconscious (1970)

* Paul MacLean's theory of the triune brain (1973)

* Miguel Sabido's own theory of soap opera tones
  (See Singhal and Rogers, 1999:62)

Their application to Indian soap opera based on the Sabido technique is discussed later. Not only is there a Formative Evaluation as indicated earlier on, but also a Summative Evaluation to assess whether audience members change as a result of exposure to entertainment-education programmes. A content analysis of a random sample of 500 letters written by *Hum Log* viewers was reported by Brown (1992) (see Chapter 3 for further details).

CHAPTER 2

The development of television in India

This chapter is in two parts. The first outlines the development of state television in India. It is not my purpose to provide a detailed chronological account of the development of television in India (for detailed accounts see Doordarshan, 1999; Luthra, 1986; Mitra, 1993; Gupta, 1998; Ninan, 1995; Rajagopal, 2001; Saksena, 1996; Singhal and Rogers, 1999). In the second part the advent of Cable and Satellite Channels in the 1990s is chronicled and examined.

Although the importance of television was recognised by Nehru at the time of India's Independence in 1947, television came to India in 1959, more than two decades after it had started in developed countries. The considerable time gap in a new technology reaching India was, according to Luthra (1986), due to a general feeling among the ruling elite that television was a luxury and a very expensive medium for mass communication. A poor country like India could not, it was assumed, spend large amounts of money on television at the expense of its more pressing developmental needs.

The first television broadcast was made possible by the gift of equipment by Phillips, which had set up a closed-circuit television at an industrial exhibition organised in Delhi. According to Ninan

> When (the exhibition) was over, it (Phillips) gifted the equipment to the government. All India Radio then put together, *for the fun of it*, (emphasis added) the country's first TV Centre in Delhi, using this reconditioned equipment and a few cameras, also gifted. This was in September 1959. (1995:18)

The gifts of Phillips were supplemented by UNESCO which provided a grant of US $20,000 and in 1965 the Federal Republic of Germany provided technical and training facilities enabling the medium of television to expand. So it was a modest beginning – a makeshift studio in *Akashvani Bhavan* – the Broadcasting House – in Delhi was used for the telecast and the transmitter of 500w power had a range of about 25kms around Delhi city.

The first telecast was viewed by members of 21 tele-clubs on community TV sets provided by the government. These tele-clubs were organised in selected middle and lower middle localities of Delhi. All India Radio (AIR) – the national sound broadcasting organisation – had been entrusted with the responsibility of producing and transmitting these programmes and later a regular television studio was set up in an auditorium used for recording concerts for the National Programme of Music of AIR. Initially the transmission consisted of two one-hour programmes a week on Tuesdays and Fridays and Ninan (1995:18-19) has described how *ad hoc* and amateurish the first telecasts were.

Expansion

In October 1961 a separate segment of school television programmes, supported by grants from the Ford Foundation, was introduced in the mornings. It was only in 1965 that a regular daily service was started with a news bulletin in Hindi. In 1967, *Krishi Darshan* was introduced, a programme on agriculture and rural development.

This programme is still ongoing and has provided the model for similar programmes for other *Kendras* (TV centres). At that time hardly anyone in a village was likely to possess a TV set and the state had to take the responsibility of providing viewing facilities also. Under a project initiated by Vikram Sarabhai (a classmate of Indira Gandhi who, it is believed, influenced her about the development potential of TV and satellite programmes), eighty villages were covered with a specially prepared, twice a week, programme on agriculture related subjects. The initial study showed significant gains in knowledge levels. Of significant interest for the soaps televised on Doordarshan in the 1980s was the use of a compere to provide the communication link between the subject expert and the uneducated farmer. The compere also acted as a narrator, the traditional *Sutradhar* of the Indian stage. Each telecast was a composite programme of three to four items. Though interviews and discussions dominated, there were also field based programmes and documentary features of short duration. Folk music and folk theatre helped in providing the entertainment element. The programmes from Delhi *Kendra* concentrated on the problems of the farmers of the neighbouring districts (now part of Haryana) and the programmes were basically in Hindi with the local accent adding to the flavour. Saksena has summed up the objectives of rural programmes on TV as follows:

- To familiarise rural viewers with the latest technical and scientific know-how about farming, agricultural implements, fertilisers, good quality seeds, cottage industries, rural development, weather forecast and so on
- To provide entertainment (folk music, plays, puppet shows)
- To acquaint the audience with the importance of education, personal hygiene, health and family welfare. (1996:25)

Rural programmes continued to be prioritised in all Doordarshan centres in subsequent years.

Shortcomings

The rural programmes were managed by general programme professionals who were trained in TV production but had no specialised knowledge in agriculture or in other rural developmental issues. In radio also, this was the situation initially but later, with the establishment of 'Farm and Home' units, agricultural professionals were employed in AIR but not in television. Furthermore, television was until recently a predominantly urban medium and the programme producers also came from urban, generally upper middle class backgrounds. The agricultural programmes were watched in urban houses but there was no system for getting feedback on them. The official line was that the programmes were meant for viewing in community situations, but it was common knowledge that community sets were not being properly utilised. The *Kendras* received a great deal of fan mail but because of the high level of illiteracy in the rural areas, there were hardly any written reactions to the rural programmes.

Viewing facilities in rural India

When regular TV services were introduced in the 1960s, and throughout the next two decades, the general feeling was that TV was not the medium for the rural population, as a majority of the villagers could not afford to buy a TV set. All the efforts of the 1970s and 1980s to reach the rural population through television started with providing TV sets for community viewing. It is estimated that more than 100,000 television sets have been provided for community viewing in the rural areas and the various schemes of the central and state governments. Tamil Nadu has established a record in providing colour TV sets to each of the 35,000 villages in the state. There have been centrally sponsored schemes providing community sets to tribal areas, villages in the Kashmir valley and also the villages in the North East.

However, the data about the utilisation of these TV sets is lacking and *ad hoc* studies conducted have revealed that in the majority of the cases, the sets were not used for the purpose for which they were provided. With the rapid expansion of TV services through the installation of low power transmitters, a majority of the over 550,000 villages have come under the coverage area of Doordarshan. The cost of a black and white TV set has remained at the same level of about Rs. 2,000/ 3,000 for over two decades; but now many villagers can afford a TV set.

The urban drive

After its start in Delhi, television reached a second city, Bombay (now Mumbai) in 1972. By 1975, when television had become the most powerful communication medium in a large number of countries, just seven cities in India had television – the four metropolitan cities of Delhi, Mumbai, Madras (now Chennai) and Calcutta; Lucknow, the capital city of the largest state, Uttar Pradesh and, for strategic reasons, Amritsar and Srinagar, the cities closest to India's borders with Pakistan. More relay centres were added in the next few years and by 1980 the number of transmitters had increased to eighteen and technically television signals reached 13.5 per cent of the area where about 25 per cent of its population lived. However, the number of people who did watch television was very much lower as the number of privately owned sets was just around1.5 million for a country with a population of 683 million at that time.

Satellite Instructional Television Experiment (SITE)

Meanwhile, in 1975-76 India witnessed a unique rural social communication effort – the Satellite Instructional Television Experiment (SITE) – using ATS-6 satellite which was lent for one year by the National Aeronautical and Space Administration (NASA) of the USA. This was the first instance anywhere in the world of using the sophisticated satellite communication technology for social education. In each of the 2,400 villages spread over six states, a television set was installed, connected to a large satellite receiver dish and groups of villagers watched in the evenings a three hour composite programme in four different languages – Hindi, Oriya, Telugu and Kannada. On the same television sets school children watched educational television programmes in the morning. Through this experiment, television reached, even though for only one year, the most inaccessible and the least developed parts of the country.

Vikram Sarabhai had a dream of using satellite technology for 'leap frogging' into rapid economic growth and social transformation and SITE was the first step in that direction. According to Ninan

> In a 1969 paper prepared for an international conference, Sarabhai had spelt out his vision of what television could do for India. A national programme which would provide television to about eighty per cent of India's population during the next ten years would be of great significance to national integration, for implementing schemes of social and economic development, and for the stimulation and promotion of the electronics industry. It is of particular significance to the large population living in isolated communities... (1995:22)

When NASA withdrew the satellite after a year, the experiment was evaluated. It is clear from comments made by a number of writers (Ninan, 1995; Mitra, 1993; Gupta, 1998; Thussu, 1998; among others) that television viewing had brought little significant behavioural changes on issues that the programmes covered. There were a number of reasons for this:

- There was a significant drop in viewership once the novelty of television had worn off

- Because of the circumstances of community viewing, women in general and those in the age group of fifteen to twenty four in particular were discouraged from viewing (Gupta, 1998:23)

- There was only a very slight increase in the adoption of birth control

- Advice in crop patterns, use of pesticides and so on benefited mostly rich farmers who could buy new seeds and agricultural implements.

Some of these disappointing results were due not to SITE *per se* but to the government's shortcomings. For example, contraceptives and other aspects of family planning were not available at the primary health centres in the villages. It was also too much to expect within one year. However, what was successful was the emergence of television as a national phenomenon. The lessons learned from SITE were used by the government in designing and utilising the domestic satellite service, INSAT, launched in 1982 (Sinha, 1996 in Raboy ed).

Up to 1976 television services continued to be operated by AIR and in 1976 a separate department – Doordarshan – was set up under the Ministry of Information and Broadcasting to operate television services. The country was in a state of emergency imposed by Indira Gandhi, who saw the benefits of using television for propaganda. 1976 also saw another milestone in the development of Doordarshan: commercial advertisements were allowed on television. However, the earnings from these advertisements in the first few years were around Rs. 20 million per year, which could hardly cover even a small portion of the expenditure of Doordarshan. In 1996-2000 the commercial earnings averaged Rs. 4 billion a year, but by then the expenditure was averaging Rs.10 billion a year... I expand on this issue in Chapter 7.

Colour Television

Indian television was started in black and white, and Delhi citizens had an opportunity of seeing colour television programmes for the first time in November 1981 at an exhibition in Delhi. Some equipment brought to the exhibition was later transferred to Doordarshan, enabling the introduction of colour transmission in 1982. The Asian Games held in Delhi in 1982 provided the impetus for substantial expansion of television services. The government wanted to showcase India to other parts of the world during this international sports event and, for the first time, investments in television were given a priority from the Planning Commission. (The Planning Commission formulates the Five Year Plans and decides about allotment of funds for development for all the ministries of the government of India and also to the states and union territories).

To bring the Asian Games to the Indian viewers, low power transmitters of 100 watt power were simultaneously commissioned in twenty cities. Doordarshan covered the Asian Games quite professionally and provided recordings of the events to 21 countries and the coverage of the Asian Games is still one of the high points in the history of Doordarshan. The next decade saw rapid development of television services in the country and by 1990 there were more than 500 transmitters spread over all parts of the country. The number of homes with television increased from 1.5 million in 1980 to over 30 million by 1990. In the sixth Five Year Plan (1980-85) the total allocation for the development of Doordarshan was Rs.1.36 billion and in the Seventh Five Year Plan (1985-90) it increased to Rs.7.2 billion – almost a six fold increase (Doordarshan, 2000).

Television Software

Most of the developing countries imported both the hardware and software for television from developed countries. India also started television services importing the television technology, studio and transmitting equipment and television receiver sets from the West but simultaneously encouraged indigenous production of equipment as well as television receiver sets. In software, India was unique – it started with indigenous software without depending on programmes developed by other countries.

In the initial telecasts of sixty minutes introduced in 1959, forty minutes were devoted to programmes of social education and 20 minutes to entertainment programmes – all produced in-house. Social education programmes were mostly 'live' discussions involving three or four participants in the studio whereas entertainment programmes were filmed in advance. By the end of the 1980s each television centre was putting out about twenty-five hours of programmes a week in the evenings and about three hours of educational television programmes for telecast in school hours. Except for a feature film in Hindi at the weekend, all the software was produced by Doordarshan professionals using the cameras, recorders, edit suites and so on which were made available in the television centres.

National and Regional Segments

Initially all the seven Doordarshan *Kendras* were producing all their software in the language and idiom of the area in which they were located, and, in a multilingual country like India, it was the only way of reaching the people. With the availability of indigenous space technology through INSAT satellites in 1982, a component of National Programmes originated from Delhi for simultaneous relay by all the transmitters of the network. The National Programmes were initially for 90 minutes each day, with two news bulletins – one in English and the other in Hindi – and the rest for current affairs, documentaries on major development projects, providing information on subjects of interest to the all-India audience. Only later was an element of entertainment included, which developed over time to a daily 30 minute slot of television drama.

Gupta (1998:42-43) has provided insightful comments on the introduction and nation-wide beaming of National Programmes. The objectives of these programmes were twofold:

- To promote national integration
- To stimulate appreciation of India's artistic and cultural heritage

In the words of Saksena, who was working in Doordarshan when national programmes were introduced:

> The introduction of National Programmes in 1982 was in itself a positive step towards accelerating the process of national integration. It was an attempt to present through TV a composite national picture and perspective of India's rich cultural heritage and diverse thinking... All the items that go in National Programme are so selected as to represent various regions and cultural expressions and activities belonging to different parts of India. (1996:12-13)

Doordarshan tried to build a consensual cultural narrative of the nation of India, in line with Nehru's motto of 'Unity in Diversity'. This diversity has often been manifested in strong assertions of their identities by linguistic, communal and subregional groups and many such assertions have resulted in organised violence. In this background, the first priority set for radio in independent India was achieving national integration and ensuring communal harmony. However, according to Gupta (1998:40-43), these attempts were unsuccessful and she lists a number of reasons, including the following:

- Doordarshan has always tended to privilege only narrow and limited group interests
- In the wake of the separatist and regionalist movements of the late 1970s and 1980s in Punjab, Assam and other places, promoting national integrity had become imperative (Gupta, 1998:43). However, Doordarshan's ethos was seen as the imposition of Hindi and a North Indian culture.

This was opposed by parties such as the DMK and the AIADMK of South India.

There was resistance to

- Doordarshan's insistence of presenting the ruling Congress Party as the true political party of India
- Occasionally, there was the anomalous situation when viewers, for example in Kerala, a south Indian state growing mostly rice, had to watch agricultural programmes meant for farmers of Haryana, a major wheat growing state adjoining Delhi.

Finance for Broadcasting

Broadcasting needs enough funds for continuing already existing operations and for future development. Furthermore, the technology of broadcasting has to be constantly upgraded to cope with rapid changes in the field of electronics. In countries where the broadcasting system is managed by private enterprise such as the USA, the cost of running the system has to come from the commercial revenues broadcasts can generate. When broadcasting is controlled by the State, it is financed through budgetary allocations. In Britain and other European countries, there is a system of licensing of radio and television sets, which generates revenue for broadcasting.

In Britain each household with a colour television paid around US$150 (£100) per year in 1999 for a licence. In India the cost of a colour set is around US $100 and a black and white set could be purchased for as little as US $30, but many Indian families have not been able to afford even this much for a television set. So the scope for generating funds through licensing has always been very limited, as the majority of the people have low incomes and cannot afford even a small percentage of what British citizens in the United Kingdom pay.

A system of licensing radio sets was introduced during British rule and television sets were also brought under licensing, but in 1984 this system was discontinued on the grounds that it was not generating sufficient revenue and at many centres the amount collected fell short of the cost of collection.

Broadcast for Development

When India went for massive development and social change through its Five Year Plans, the public service function of radio was redefined to include popularising the Plan schemes. Separate units were set up in all major AIR stations to highlight the objectives of the Five Year Plans and the achievements made through these Plans. Emphasis was given to issues such as raising agricultural production, improving the status of public health, including a scientific awareness among the people, involving women in a significant way in nation-building activities.

Media always provides a platform for a dialogue between the government and its people and radio did provide that platform. However, in the course of time, there was less dialogue and more 'talking to'; programmes which should have been interactive were instead dull talks from officials at various levels. The increasing use of radio to counter political opposition during Indira Gandhi's rule gave rise to snide remarks that AIR had become All Indira Radio.

The programming policies of Doordarshan were much the same. To justify investments from the state, Doordarshan had to give more importance to education and information and there was little entertainment. Programme producers mostly came from the elite sections of society and were more interested in getting feedback from their peer groups than in meeting the entertainment needs of the general viewers.

The weekly feature film on television was the only entertainment, which appealed to the masses. Doordarshan produced other entertainment programmes using drama and music formats, but these were generally 'highbrow' – the adaptation of literary works to television – and programmes based on musical compositions set to dance.

Amrita Shah has described the television content of those days as follows:

> There were quiz shows, Origami lessons, How-to-do-it yourself, Bonsai and wild life... and Cricket matches... Dreams, however, are prone to fade. And nothing fades faster than novelty... Once we had grown accustomed to its blinking visage we were bored – the unglamorous visuals began to seem un-utterably dreary... But crucially once we had stopped exclaiming over the wonders of the medium we realised there was nothing to watch. A large part of the limited broadcast was taken up by educational programmes. These were of poor quality and clearly of little relevance to the actual audience... As the 70s came to an end television viewers were a disgruntled lot. Like suitors in haste, we had looked long and hard on the object of our passion and found it wanting. What we had was not enough. We wanted more. (1997:5-6)

Shah was living in Mumbai (Bombay) and could have also watched programmes in Marathi put out by Bombay Doordarshan *Kendra*. One can only imagine the plight of viewers in, say, Kerala. There were no programmes in their language and for them television was only a facility for watching, once a week, a film without going to the cinema hall. Television was promoted as the medium of information (and education), but the information was not in Malayalam, which they understood, but in a language alien to them. It was only in 1991 that most television viewers in Kerala could watch programmes in Malayalam, but by then they had become accustomed to treat television as a theatre at home.

The advent of cable and satellite television and their impact on Doordarshan

The Gulf War of January 1991 ushered in a new era of television in many parts of the world. Ted Turner's Cable News Network (CNN) brought vivid pictures of the war, or those aspects of the war the USA wanted people to see, 'live' to the drawing rooms of everyone who had access to CNN all over the world. In India this CNN coverage was witnessed by a select few, though not in their homes but in metropolitan cities where the American Embassy, its consulates or the United States Information Centres had made arrangements for viewing CNN. In addition, some of the five star hotels set up special dish antennae to catch CNN signals from the distant satellites. Though just a few thousand Indians might have watched the CNN coverage of the Gulf War, there were elaborate newspaper reports on the excitement of the war being brought live to the audiences, and people suddenly woke up to the possibilities of foreign television programmes being beamed through satellites to Indian homes.

Cable Television

While satellite television was a novelty in 1991, cable television, an alternative or supplement to Doordarshan, had already started growing. When Indian television shifted to colour transmission in 1982, there were only a few thousand colour television sets in the country. Many of those were brought by Indians returning from abroad, mostly from the Gulf countries. The Indian government was keen that the newly introduced colour telecasts should be widely viewed and allowed the import of colour television kits from Korea by manufacturers of black and white television sets. Simultaneously the government lowered the duty on colour television sets and video cassette recorders (VCRs) brought by Indians returning from their visits abroad. Initially ownership of VCRs was confined to rich households, but soon small-scale entrepreneurs found a business opportunity in them. Many Indians watched feature films obsessively and repeatedly. Famous artist M.F. Hussain has admitted to having watched the 1998 feature film, *Hum Aapke Hain Kaun* (Who am I to you) starring Madhuri Dixit more than thirty times. Video cassettes of many popular films were being released, mostly for the foreign markets. In India the market for these cassettes was too restricted, as few people owned VCRs.

Young entrepreneurs started investing in VCRs and set up video 'parlours' where people could watch film cassettes for a small fee. This concept was gradually extended to renting out VCRs (sometimes along with a colour television set) with cassettes. Even people living in shanties were soon hiring cassettes – often a dozen – to watch along with family and friends over the weekend. These video libraries mushroomed in the mid-1980s, in large towns and small. Cable television was a further extension of the video library concept. Small operators connected a number of houses in their neighbourhoods, starting in crowded localities through cables and playing back videos of films (and occasionally other programmes) according to a fixed schedule. Subscribers and their families could watch four or five films at convenient hours every day and many calculated that this was less expensive than paying for admission to cinema halls. This was a real bonanza for those fed on the only-once-a-week quota of feature films on Doordarshan. The clientele for cable television increased in large towns and small. The concept of cable television was quickly picked up in Gujarat and Maharashtra where there was local entrepreneurship and also a craze for Hindi feature films. Before long, it reached cities in other states like Tamil Nadu and Andra Pradesh – states where films, apart from entertaining the masses, also played a crucial role in state politics (see for example Pandian, 1992).

At first patronage for cable television was limited to the middle and the lower middle class homes for two reasons. Firstly, films had great appeal to them and secondly, cable operation was more economical in crowded localities. The investments needed to reach a sizeable number of houses in densely populated areas were minimal and even with a clientele of a hundred or two hundred houses the cable operator could make a profit (Doordarshan, 1997). Cable television started around 1984 but soon spread and by 1990 it had reached cities in all parts of the country.

Star Television

Around the time that CNN was covering the 1991 Gulf War, a powerful satellite, Asiasat-1, with footprints covering most of Asia and parts of Africa, was launched in Hong Kong. Richard Li, son of Hong Kong's richest man Li Ka-Shing, had hired seven C-band transponders on this satellite to launch STAR – Satellite Television Service for the Asian Region (Shah, 1997). China and India, the two largest countries in Asia, had been considered as the prospective markets for Star Television. The focus was on China rather than India, with English programmes dubbed into Mandarin. However, contrary to expectations, STAR initially received an enthusiastic reception in India and faced serious problems in China. The existing cable networks in India needed only a small dish antenna to distribute programmes beamed from Hong Kong to their subscribers. According to the Audience Research Unit of Doordarshan (Doordarshan, 1999), India already had a base of 30 million television homes – the result of rapid expansion of terrestrial television by Doordarshan. Also the cable television industry was growing rapidly in urban areas.

In August 1991, Star television began transmissions with four channels beamed from Hong Kong. Star Plus provided general entertainment programmes in English including American soap operas like *Santa Barbara* and *The Bold and the Beautiful*. The others were Music television – MTV, BBC World Service and Prime Sports. English programme channels were not expected to have mass appeal, but the programmes did interest certain sections of the population. A survey commissioned by Star television and conducted by FSA, a market research company in Australia, revealed that by February 1993 the number of homes receiving Star television had increased to 3.3.million (Doordarshan, 1996).

However, a more comprehensive survey conducted by Doordarshan around the same time among 6,000 cable connected households in ten cities had found that even in most of the homes receiving Star channels, the main viewing of the VCR channel of the cable operator and the Star television programmes recorded very low viewership (Doordarshan, 1996).

The situation changed after the introduction of ZeeTV on the Star platform and the opening of channels in regional languages in the South. What Star television achieved was a new market. A few educated women were tracking the fortunes of the characters in *Santa Barbara*, young people watched MTV and men claimed they watched BBC news bulletins, but the audience of Star channels formed only a tiny percentage of the total Indian television audience.

The promoters of Star television failed to obtain the type of advertising they were hoping for. In 1993, Rupert Murdoch's News Corporation purchased Star television from the Hong Kong industrialist, but Star continued to be a loss-making venture for a long while. In the mid 1990s Star television switched from a pan-Asian English language format to a strategy of providing Asian language programmes (Herman and McChesney, 1997:73). As part of this strategy, Star Plus became a hybrid channel of English and Hindi and Channel V, which had by then replaced MTV, 'Indianised' most of its programmes – which meant including songs from Hindi films.

Zee Television

ZeeTV, the general entertainment satellite channel, launched in October 1992 on the Star platform, was the first transnational channel and it proved a big success within a year. When ZeeTV was launched, another Hindi satellite channel – ATN operating from a Russian satellite was already available to Indian audiences. This channel, launched on 15 August 1992, was telecasting Hindi feature films and programmes based on songs from these films. ATN Channel did not develop any character of its own – it did not have any Unique Selling Proposition (USP) and ZeeTV, though the second Hindi Channel, reaped all the benefits of being the first entrant to a virgin field.

ZeeTV was a joint venture of Star television and Subash Chandra of Essel Industries. According to Ninan, 'Chandra's background was a combination of making money through wheeling and dealing, and dabbling in innovations before the market was quite ready for them' (1995:161). Although Chandra had no previous experience in media, he risked investing 5 million US dollars for a fifty per cent share for a Hindi satellite channel on the Star platform.

Impact of ZeeTV on Doordarshan

Star television had given a certain prestige for having a cable connection, but it was ZeeTV that made satellite television programmes extremely popular with the upper middle and middle classes in northern and western India. These two areas, with the metropolitan cities of Mumbai, Delhi and Ahmedabad and the economically well-off states of Punjab, Haryana, Maharasthra and Gujarat accounted for about 70 per cent of the total consumer market for India. With its effective marketing ZeeTV managed to obtain a big share of the advertising money.

ZeeTV took away a big chunk of advertising from Doordarshan by taking advantage of the known weaknesses of a government department. Doordarshan had gone commercial as early as 1976, but never even thought of establishing a separate division to market its programmes. Indeed, *Prasar Bharati* (Broadcasting Corporation of India) took a decision to establish a combined marketing Division for AIR and Doordarshan and the first office of the Division was inaugurated in Mumbai in 2001. Both AIR and Doordarshan had nothing more than sales units, which sold airtime to only those who approached them. They had rigid rules about the rates to be charged for sponsorship and advertising spots. Doordarshan had a highly centralised set up which hindered programming decisions. By introducing sponsored programmes in an *ad hoc* manner, Doordarshan had virtually lost control over programmes telecast on its own channels. The success of ZeeTV dented Doordarshan's monopolist control. The senior management of Doordarshan went on the defensive to protect the airwaves against what they considered cheap and vulgar programmes dished out by transnational satellite networks. Indeed, in the words of Mankekar

> By that point (1997), Doordarshan was engaged in a serious battle with Zee, Star and the Sony Entertainment Network. At stake once again was culture: the identities, aspirations, and fantasies of Indian viewers; the consumer practices of the ever-expanding middle classes; discursive practices of masculinity, femininity, and sexuality; constructions of personal and collective memory. (1999:336-337)

Fears about this cultural invasion from the satellite channels centred around the Americanisation of the Indian way of life. A clear distinction emerged between the aims, objectives and content of the programmes on Doordarshan and those on the satellite channels, particularly ZeeTV. However, ATN did not develop any philosophy of its own and ZeeTV stepped in with a completely different approach from not only Doordarshan but also the other satellite channels. ZeeTV also depended on films, but additionally it had game shows, chat shows, soap operas and some new formats of current affairs programmes.

Targeting the affluent upper middle and middle classes of northern and western India, ZeeTV's presentations had a new format characterised by 'loud, friendly or even sarcastic' presenters (Shah, 1997). For example, there was a current affairs programme – *Janata Ki Adalat* (The Court of the People) where Rajat Sharma interviewed senior politicians of the country, asking very awkward questions in a friendly and affable manner. The audience enjoyed watching the discomfiture of the politicians who were, in turn, happy to reach a very large audience.

A new *lingua franca* emerged. ZeeTV uses a language nearer to the street language or 'kitty party' language which later came to be known as Hinglish or sometimes

Zinglish (Thussu, 2000), a curious mixture of Hindi and English. The purists felt that this was a 'bastardisation' of Hindi. The media, particularly the print media, has always been supportive of Indian languages. But while the English press in India has always been particular about style, English grammar and syntax, the same elite appear happy with the new Hindi of ZeeTV, which broke all accepted language norms. One explanation offered by Page and Crawley is that Hinglish has caught on with the urban young all over North India... 'ZeeTV's Hinglish also questioned the hegemony of language. The highly sanitised Hindi and the very formal English... took a beating with the coming of Zee' (2001:156-157).

ZeeTV differed from Doordarshan in content too. According to Ninan (1995), ZeeTV showed no misery compared to the dreary image portrayed by Doordarshan. For example, Bhagwanti of *Hum Log* lived in a 'Janata flat' – a cubby hole in one of those drab apartment blocks built on a mass scale for the low income groups by the government. She wore cheap cotton sarees and her daughters had to make do with inexpensive clothing and had no time to worry about make-up and hairstyles. But ZeeTV characters live in beautiful bungalows with expensive furniture and at any time of the day they wear heavy makeup and designer clothes. Doordarshan was trying to cater to the masses and especially to the under-privileged in its public service broadcasting, but ZeeTV marketed its programmes to consumers and particularly those who had enough purchasing power. ZeeTV came to India when the country was opening itself to the world market. People were disillusioned with the Nehruvian model of public ownership of all the vital sectors, which had created what is described as the 'licence-quota-permit-raj'. (This term is used to describe the 'ponderous network of official and unofficial clearances required to set up a business in India, repatriate profits, import or export commodities etc'. (Thomas, 1993:71 note 7). It became synonymous with bureaucratic corruption. Liberalisation and globalisation had become the new mantra, private enterprise was being openly welcomed by the government and ZeeTV was a symbol of this enterprise culture for the middle and upper classes.

State-controlled and strait-jacketed, Doordarshan was unable to meet the needs of this new situation. At the time that satellite channels were introduced in India, Doordarshan was facing a major internal crisis. All the serials telecast on Doordarshan in the 1980s turned out to be money spinners and this created fierce competition among private producers to obtain a slot on Doordarshan. Producers started using their connections in political parties to get preferential treatment on Doordarshan. Charges and counter charges of corruption were made and the Ministry of Information and Broadcasting which controlled Doordarshan announced a scheme in 1990 under which anyone with or without any knowledge of software production could apply for a slot on Doordarshan.

Not only was the scheme a disaster but it led to court action. The only source of entertainment programmes for Doordarshan was completely blocked while court proceedings were in progress. Additionally, there was labour trouble inside Doordarshan and in 1992-93 when satellite television was making inroads, the professionals in Doordarshan had their hands tied and were in no position to react.

However, the senior management of Doordarshan tried to take on the satellite channels by starting five satellite channels of its own, one to compete with ZeeTV and the other four to take on Star television. The programme output of Doordarshan *Kendras* was then about 400 hours a week. Overnight and with no additional funding, Doordarshan was asked to generate an extra 400 hours. The scheme was doomed to failure and only one of the five channels, Metro entertainment, achieved success.

The real challenge for Doordarshan was to provide more entertainment programmes for the upwardly mobile sections of the population which, according to Chandrasekhar (1999), were shifting their loyalties to satellite channels. The Metro entertainment channel started in 1993 by linking up the four terrestrial transmitters Doordarshan had set up in late 1980s in four metropolitan cities, and the programmes were also made available for cable operators to distribute on their networks. By 1994, the terrestrial transmission of Metro Channel was extended to twenty cities which together with the four metropolitan cities, accounted for about 30 per cent of the television homes in the country – well beyond the reach registered by the most popular satellite channel. These cities also had a higher percentage of upper income group households, the target of the satellite channels. Equally important was the strategy of Metro Channel to provide the same type of programme as the satellite channels. One of its main offerings was soap operas – slick in presentation and racy in style, with unexpected twists and turns in each episode.

By 1999, the development of television channels was staggering. There were ten general entertainment channels in Hindi, about 30 general entertainment channels in regional languages and more than 50 thematic channels. Within just a decade, a variety of channels were fighting one another for a share of viewership, a slice of advertisement and the additional revenues from subscription. The targets of the television channels were the 362 million people (April 1999) who had television in their homes and a further 120 million who watched television in their neighbours' homes or in community centres. However, among the 362 million who had access to television, only about 120-130 million could watch channels other than Doordarshan. But ZeeTV has certain advantages over Doordarshan. Although it addressed the Indian audience, it was promoted as a South Asian Channel. There was a sizeable population of sub-continental expatriates in the Gulf countries and the Hindi programmes of ZeeTV appealed to them.

ZeeTV also claimed viewers in Pakistan, Nepal, Bangladesh and Sri Lanka. In recent years it has extended its operation to the United States and countries such as Mauritius where there are sizeable expatriate populations. For example, in the United Kingdom, ZeeTV claimed a subscription base of 166,000 homes in 1999 (Press Release of ZeeTV issued in 1999). ZeeTV has become the channel for India's diaspora.

Other Hindi Channels

Impressed by the success of ZeeTV, a number of Indian and foreign players entered the Indian market. Sony Entertainment Television (SET), Joint America India Network of Jain television were the main Hindi Channels to follow ZeeTV.

Sony invested generously in quality software and offered strong competition and at times its audience share topped ZeeTV. In the first reincarnation of Star Plus a good number of Hindi programmes, produced at considerable expense, were introduced. Star Plus also had news bulletins in Hindi and English, produced by the prestigious company, New Delhi Television. Some of these programmes did become popular, but STAR failed in its main objective: to attract viewers from ZeeTV. In 2000, Star television adopted a new strategy, turning Star Plus into a one hundred per cent Hindi Channel. All English programmes, including the nine o'clock English news which had brought prestige to STAR, were moved to Star World. One of the newly introduced game shows *Kaun Banega Crorepathi* (Who wants to be a millionaire?) following an internationally successful formula was an instant hit. Many other serials like *Sans Bhi Kabhi Bahu Thi* (mother-in-law was once daughter- in-law), *Kahani Ghar Ghar Ki* (the story of every home) also attracted huge viewership and for the first time since its existence ZeeTV lost its leading position among Hindi Channels.

SUN Television

The success of ZeeTV opened opportunities for starting channels in other languages, particularly the languages of South India. In a way, there was greater demand for these, as Doordarshan was generally perceived in some parts of India as promoting Hindi at the expense of regional languages. The breakdown of the USSR had freed many transponders on Russian satellites, which were used mainly to gain the signals of the Western satellites. New players could use the transponders of these satellites.

SUN television, with programmes exclusively in Tamil, began its transmissions on the Tamil New Year day in 1993. This was the first private satellite channel in an Indian language other than Hindi. Initially, it depended wholly on films and film-based programmes but it soon commissioned a few Game shows.

Kalanidhi Maran, a non-resident Indian business executive promoted SUN tele-vision. He is the son of Murasoli Maran, a Minister in the Union Cabinet and nephew of M.Karunanidhi, thrice Chief Minister of Tamil Nadu and unchallenged leader of DMK, a leading Dravidian Party. Tamil Nadu politicians have effcctively used films and newspapers and continued this tradition and SUN television was soon used for political ends. In the general elections of 1996 to the Parliament and Tamil Nadu Assembly, DMK encouraged by the political awareness raised by SUN television (see Page and Crawley, 2001:79) trounced its main opposition party AIADMK. In 2001, when DMK was in opposition, coverage by SUN television of the arrest of Karunanidhi changed the political face of Tamil Nadu. SUN television gradually extended its activities to other South Indian States. It purchased Gemini television, a moderately successful Telugu Channel. It started UDAYA, a satellite channel in Kannada and SURYA, a satellite channel in Malayalam. With all these channels it is in a position to offer advertisers attractive packages for the whole of the South, and the SUN empire is now one of the most prosperous enterprises in India.

Other Channels

The success of SUN television has inspired many others to start satellite channels in different languages. In Tamil, only *Raj* television and *Vijay* television im-mediately followed SUN. Owing to political factors, AIADMK has its own channel – JJTV (JAYA television) launched in 1995. In neighbouring Andra Pradesh news-paper publisher Ramoji Rao started the Telugu Channel, *Eenadu* in 1995, and under the brand name he set up *Eenadu* channels in Bengali, Kannada, Marathi and Urdu. In Karnataka there are two other channels – *Kaveri* and *Suprabatha*, apart from *Udaya* and *Eenadu*. In Kerala, Asia network, the Communist Party of India (Marxists) and two others run separate Malayalam channels. Elsewhere in India, there are three to five channels in Bengali, Marathi, Gujarati and Punjabi. Some channels in Tamil, Telugu and Kannada have been commercial successes but there have also been failures, such as Jain TV, NEPC TV and Home TV.

Thematic Channels

When Star television started beaming into India with four channels, it also brought to India for the first time the concept of thematic channels —- channels specialising in one specific area. BBC was the round-the-clock news and current affairs channel, Prime Sports covered only sports and MTV was the channel of popular Western music. Under Rupert Murdoch, Star television set up Star Movies in 1994 – an English movie channel, the first encrypted channel. All these channels targeted niche audiences but had little Indian content. The vast majority of viewers, even among the small section that had access to these channels, did not show much interest in these channels. However, in the last few years, thematic channels with Indian content are available and some have established a small but loyal viewership.

ZeeTV's channel – Zee Movies became the first thematic channel of Indian content. Star also started 'Star News' just before the Parliamentary elections in 1998, a round-the-clock news channel with programmes produced by an Indian company, New Delhi Television. ZeeTV also began its own news and current affairs channel. Discovery Channel broadcasting programmes on wild life and geography targeted another niche and has been joined by National Geographic Channel. These channels are widely considered educational and children are encouraged to watch them.

Cable and Satellite Television

At the beginning of 1991, India had only one national channel and people were craving more television entertainment. A decade later the position has drastically changed (see page 21). The major cable networks in large cities are now providing their subscribers with about one hundred cable and satellite channels and even people living in smaller cities have the choice of twenty to thirty channels. These channels fight one another for a share of viewership, a slice of the advertising cake and additional revenues from subscription.

But this is only one part of the big picture. India's billion people live in about 190 million homes – the National Readership Survey conducted in 2001 (Reports of National Readership Survey, 2001) estimates that about 58 percent of these homes still do not have television sets and in rural areas only 35 per cent do. Cable has grown substantially in urban areas and in rural areas of South India.

There are major variations from state to state. In the Punjab, even in rural areas, nearly 65 percent of homes own television sets whereas in Bihar the TV ownership in urban areas is 58 percent and in rural areas it is as low as ten percent. In prosperous Punjab only twelve percent of rural TV homes have access to cable whereas in Andhra it is 88 percent.

Regulation and control

Democratic countries allegedly respect freedom of expression for their citizens and generally do not interfere in the media of their country. At the same time, every government accepts its duty to protect vulnerable sections of society whose interests may be affected because of the absence of a forum for their involvement. Governments encourage the setting up of autonomous regulatory bodies which draw up codes covering issues like programming for children, proper representation to minorities, assurance of a minimum percentage for local programming, the quantum and nature of commercial advertisements, timings of broadcasts of programmes unsuitable for children. Many countries have also taken steps to protect the interests of public service broadcasters against the onslaught of commercial broadcasters.

In India, the Cabinet has completely barred foreign print media. In the last decade, there has been liberalisation in every field, but direct foreign investment is still prohibited. However, even after a decade, foreign satellite channels are still free for all and anybody can broadcast anything. The Ministry of Information and Broadcasting had appointed a committee to suggest a policy on controlling or regulating satellite television. The committee rightly concluded that technologically it would be impossible to stop the signals reaching India but unfortunately, it did not even consider the possibilities of regulating the ground distribution of these channels.

Cable networks have been mushrooming since the mid 1980s and there have always been doubts about whether these operations were legal, but the government took no action to regulate cable operations. Even under the laws then prevailing it would have been possible in the initial stages to regulate ground distribution by franchising different areas to different companies. The government could have earned significant funds to spend on public service broadcasting.

Only after Star television announced that it would be starting an encrypted channel of English movies in 1994, did the government take some action. India has strict rules about feature films, censoring scenes of sex and violence, which could have adverse effects on children. There was a general feeling that a foreign channel showing uncensored films to Indian viewers would undermine the very process of censorship. The government hurriedly issued an ordinance (later replaced by an Act in 1995, the Cable Television Network Regulation Act) prescribing a code for programmes and commercial advertisements on encrypted channels distributed by cable television operators.

The free-to-air C-band channels, which accounted for over 95 percent of viewership, were not covered in the Act and more importantly cable operators never took this Act seriously. The Cable Television Network Regulation Act has been amended to include provisions for compulsory relay of three channels of Doordarshan, but it is still toothless – violations of the Act cannot be punished.

The Cricket Association of Bengal and the Board of Control for cricket in India had meanwhile filed a petition in the Supreme Court of India against the Government for refusing permission to a foreign satellite company to directly telecast some cricket matches organised by them. The Supreme Court of India delivered a judgement on this petition in February 1995 wherein it ruled that a citizen has a fundamental right to use the best means of imparting and receiving information and to have telecasting for this purpose. The Court also said that the Central Government should take immediate steps to establish an independent autonomous public authority representative of all sections and interests in the society to control and regulate the use of the airwaves (see Page and Crawley, 2001:269-270).

When the Supreme Court delivered this judgement, the central government was controlling AIR and Doordarshan. Broadcasting, at least in the legal sense, was still a monopoly of the Government. However, from 1991 onwards, Indian viewers have been exposed to the programmes of the various satellites beamed from different countries. The Government had not allowed the linking up of programmes from India but there were no restrictions on receiving programmes from outside India.

The real challenge for Doordarshan was to provide more entertainment programmes for the upwardly mobile and modern sectors of the population as they shifted their loyalties to satellite channels (Chandrasekhar, 1999). Metro Channel did quite well, at least in the initial stages, providing the same type of programmes as the satellite channels. There was *Superhit Muqabla*, a countdown of Hindi film songs presented in the style of MTV VJs, which even satellite channels had considered too far ahead of the times. The Metro Channel also had game shows, soap operas and other programmes similar to those on satellite channels.

By the end of 1995 DD-1, the primary service of Doordarshan devoted to public service broadcasting, had joined the Metro Channel DD-2 in the competition for viewership with afternoon serials, Count Down programmes, game shows and so on. There was little difference between Doordarshan and the other satellite channels. In the late 1980s Doordarshan had used entertainment programmes to carry social messages based on the entertainment-education communication strategy. With the advent of satellite channels and persistent demands from the government to generate internal revenue, Doordarshan was forced to abandon its goals of public service broadcasting and join the mainstream. The next chapter examines some examples of non-conventional and conventional soap operas on Doordarshan.

CHAPTER 3

Soap operas telecast on Doordarshan

Recently the number of soap operas telecast on Indian television and satellite channels has proliferated, especially on ZeeTV. ZeeTV is the only satellite channel whose soap operas are considered in this study.

The first soap opera – *Hum Log* (We People) based on the Sabido's Entertainment – Education Communication Strategy was telecast in 1984 on Doordarshan. Its phenomenal success led to a series of soap operas particularly with the advent of satellite television in 1990s.

In1990 Indian viewers had only Doordarshan telecasting about one hour of entertainment programmes a day. These were mainly serials and sitcoms, but by 2000 there were at least ten Hindi general entertainment channels including DD-1 and DD-2, providing many hours of drama-based programmes every day for Indian viewers. This included about 50 soap operas in Hindi, some stretching to five episodes a week.

What is noteworthy is the number of soap operas telecast and also their huge range of theme and content. Broadly speaking, Indian soap operas can be classified as follows:

Religious	• *Ramayan* and *Mahabharat*
Political/Militaristic	• *Param Veer Chakra* (*PVC*) – the highest military decoration for service in combat.[1]
	• *Tamas* (darkness) – Partition and the birth of the nation of India
Social/Cultural	• *Hum Log* (We People) family planning/family drama
	• *Humraahi* (Fellow Traveller)
	• *Rajani*
	• *Buniyaad* (The Foundation)
	• *Udaan I and II* (Flight)
	• *Yugantar*

Soap operas have characters that are 'real' in the sense that viewers feel involved with their affairs, but they generally depict a world far removed from that of most viewers. This imaginary world, though, is a preferable one to viewers for many reasons. Arsenault (1999) identified some of the features of this world as follows:

- **Lovers** Never a lack of a lover or spouse. If someone is single s/he won't stay that way.

- **Even larger families** Soap families are never complete. Forgotten or 'surprise' children show up unexpectedly. Unplanned pregnancies, long lost relatives keep turning up.

- **Illness** Life threatening diseases or injuries are cured or healed within months or even days. Things that would kill or disable a 'real' human rarely do so to soap characters.

- **Courts** Indian courts may not deliver justice fast but soaps record witnesses, cross-examination, arguments and judgement, all in one day.

- **Employment** If you want a job, you will get one in no time. The pay is always excellent and the atmosphere in any office extremely pleasant. You do not have to commute to office – the boss will pick you up.

- **Telephones** They always work. The party is always ready on the other side to receive your call, dressed in her/his best clothes.

- **Police** There is always a family member or close friend in the police force. So if you're ever arrested you know you'll be dealt with fairly. All policemen are polite and the officers are always young and handsome.

- **Medical care** Hospitals always attend to patients immediately. The doctors are waiting and the operating theatres are ready for the most complex surgery.

- **Community relations** Everyone knows everybody else. No matter how remote the connection, everyone ends up together at functions and gatherings, or working together in the same business.

- **Financial worries** Soap opera characters hardly ever have to pay for anything and always have money for any emergency. Somehow even the poorest members of a community are able to afford the best.

- **Beautiful people** There is hardly an ugly face. Characters are not just beautiful but brainy. They also become heads of large enterprises and can manage any crisis.

- **Death** Death does not mean 'forever'. If a character dies, s/he can come back from the dead, become a twin or long lost relative, or survive in ghostly form.

- **Murder** There is never a shortage of murderers in any fictional town. When one murderer is disposed of, another immediately takes her/his place.

- **Ageing** One can age overnight. Ageing means a few streaks of silver hair and the same healthy body.

- **Accidents** An accident is always waiting to happen. But if you are involved in an accident, you will end up with a neat bandage which can be removed next day.

Soap operas on Doordarshan certainly have many of the features listed above. But, as is shown in Chapter 4, they characterise ZeeTV soap operas since they are essentially entertainment, much like those on US television.

During1985-1990 Doordarshan used soap operas to carry pro-developmental messages. It was trying to do three things:

- Increase the entertainment content of its programmes without diluting its avowed objective of social education

- Bring in producers from outside Doordarshan who could invest in quality programmes

- Increase the commercial earnings of the network

Hum Log (We People) was the first Indian soap opera to try and meet all these criteria. It was telecast for 17 months (from 1984 to 1985) – a total of 156 episodes, each twenty minutes long. The twenty minute time frame was set as Doordarshan wanted to allow about seven minutes for commercial spots – about two minutes for the sponsor and five for other advertisers. The sponsor paid for the cost of production and also a small fee to Doordarshan and was compensated by the two minutes' free advertisement time. The rest earned substantial income for Doordarshan from other advertisers.

The plot of *Hum Log* centred around the joys and sorrows of a lower-middle class family living in a housing colony built by the government for the under-privileged. The Rams were an extended family of three generations living together, typical of many Indian households and this is illustrated in the diagram on page 30.

Bhagwanti, the self-effacing, quiet woman who attends to the needs of the whole family, represented the middle generation. She suffered at the hands of her husband and her mother-in-law. She was a stereotype of the traditional Indian wife-mother. Her husband, Basesar Ram was boorish, addicted to drink and showed scant consideration for his wife and children. Basesar's father, Riijak, was a World War veteran and a strict disciplinarian. He was hardworking and represented the high moral values of the generation that was fading out. His wife, the once beautiful

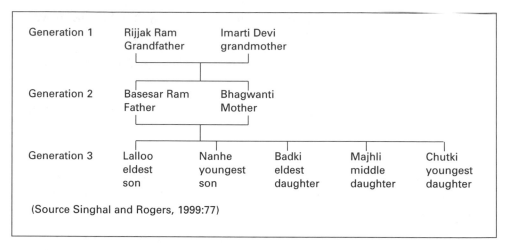

(Source Singhal and Rogers, 1999:77)

Imarti Devi, was a deeply indulgent grandmother who could be selfish and sarcastic at times.

Bhagwanti had five children – three daughters and two sons. The three daughters each represented the emerging generation of women. The eldest, Badki, was proficient in sewing, worked hard and later married a medical doctor. She was a positive role model of female equality. The second daughter, Majhli, a failure in school, was beautiful and glamour-struck. She runs away trying to make it in the Bombay film industry, but gets involved in the underworld – she acts the negative role model representing the pitfalls of modernity. The youngest daughter, Chutki, was a studious, no-nonsense practical girl with the clearly defined goal of becoming a doctor. The five women characters of the serial represented the various positioning of women in Indian society and the three daughters indicated some of the options available to young women in India today.

Among the sons, the elder, Lalloo was a 'country bumpkin', often the object of humour in the drama. The younger, Nanhe, wanted to get rich by whatever means possible. These two sons remained outside the main action and were only sub-plot.

Since by all accounts *Hum Log* represented a turning point in Indian television, rapidly becoming the most popular television programme in the history of Indian television (Singhal and Rogers, 1999), it has been widely discussed in the popular press, academic journals and was the subject of a doctoral dissertation by Malwade-Rangarajan in 1992.

It is interesting to examine this highly successful Indian soap opera and assess the extent to which it adhered to Miguel Sabido's entertainment-education communication strategy.

The first few episodes had disappointing ratings. Viewers were alienated by the didactic sermons about family planning, the slow development of the story line and the indifferent acting. Consequently, after the first thirteen episodes, scriptwriter Manohar Shyam Joshi did a formative evaluation (part of Sabido's communication strategy) and enlarged the scope from just family planning to issues of the status of women, family harmony, community living and so on. Each episode of *Hum Log* ended with an epilogue wherein Ashok Kumar, a well-known film star, summed up the episode. This provided viewers with appropriate guides to action in their own lives (Singhal and Rogers, 1999: 75-76). Ashok Kumar's role was similar to that of a *Sutradhar*, the narrator in traditional Sanskrit plays.

All this as well as the theoretical underpinnings of *Hum Log* is generally consistent with the methodology advocated by Sabido in his explanation of the entertainment-education communication strategy.

In *Hum Log*, therefore, the following can be seen:

Dramatic Theory is derived from Eric Bentley, a professor of theatre and drama at Columbia University. His theory describes how storytelling and drama can effectively involve an audience with a specific message. Of all the genres identified by Bentley, it was melodrama that was most powerful, since in it good and bad behaviours can be sharply contrasted. The much-maligned genre of melodrama, so typical of Indian popular culture, especially Indian popular cinema, is being valorised. In line with Sabido's arguments, the importance of drama also lends itself to a theory of tones. Sabido believes that an effective pro-development soap opera must have the same dramatic tone as a traditional commercial soap because an 'intellectualised' soap with a distinct 'educational' tone would not be popular with the public. And certainly in *Hum Log*, the early episodes were comparatively unsuccessful in engaging the audience since the tone of the soap opera was didactic and the issue of family planning too overt.

Another theoretical aspect of the entertainment-education communication strategy can be found in Jung's theory of the **collective unconscious**. The confusion that exists in modern life can be countered by implementing Jung's theory of archetypes and stereotypes. Archetypes are unconscious representations that become personified through television characters who encounter typical life situations. An archetype is a mental image of a certain type of person – the great mother, for example. Stereotypes are culturally distinct categorisations of people based on pre-judgements, imagination and insufficient information.

> The television Soap Opera is a potentially powerful vehicle for purveying myths – legends that express the beliefs of a people, often explaining natural phenomenon or the origins of a people. Myths are part of our collective un-

conscious... mythical stories represent a way in which collective ideas originating in the unconscious are passed from one generation to another through archetypes and stereotypes. (Singhal and Rogers, 1999: 64)

Thus, in *Hum Log* the characters were depicted as archetypes – Rijjak Ram, the grandfather, a self-sufficient hardworking, morally upright man is a positive role model whereas his son, Basesar Ram has a serious drinking problem, mistreats his family and is financially irresponsible – a negative role model.

Such positive and negative role models are aspects of social learning theory, of which Bandura (1977, 1986) is one of the best-known exponents. The behavioural impact of television role models is difficult to measure quantitatively and, even in the case of US soap operas, audiences can still learn from media characters. But in the case of *Hum Log*, Anil Khosla, the president of Chandigarth's youth club, wrote a letter to Ashok Kumar, explaining how his club had collected 892 names of eye donors in an eye donation campaign (Brown, 1992:162). Two assessments of the impact of *Hum Log* were carried out by Singhal and Rogers and extensively reported by them (1999: chapter four). In 1987, they surveyed 1170 adults residing in three geographical regions:

- In and around Delhi – a Hindi speaking area in North India

- In and around Pune – a Marathi speaking area in Western India near Bombay (Mumbai)

- And in and around Madras (Chennai) a Tamil speaking area in South India.

They also sent questionnaires to 321 of the 500 letter writers in August 1987, twenty months after the *Hum Log* broadcasts had ended. An analysis of a random sample of the 500 letters written by *Hum Log* viewers indicated about seven percent of letter writers reported that *Hum Log* had brought about change of some kind in their personal behaviour (Singhal and Rogers, 1989:341-342). The two authors also interviewed 25 key officials responsible for creating, maintaining and sustaining *Hum Log*. This triangulation research strategy was adopted because by the time these assessments took place the broadcasts had ended, so this strategy was intended to overcome some of the limitations of a *post hoc* evaluation of a television programme. Indeed, Singhal and Rogers (1999:97-100) state that the research design for the summative evaluation of *Hum Log* is less than perfect in that was limited by 'reliance on an *ex post facto* design' (p100).

At the time of its broadcast, *Hum Log* commanded an audience of 60 million people, the highest ever to watch a television programme in India. Naturally the audience in Delhi was the highest – 65% to 90% – and the ratings in Madras, where Hindi is not familiar, amounted to 48%.

The character the audience identified with the most was Rijjak Ram, the grand-father, and the second highest was Bhagwanti, the long-suffering mother in the family, a stereotype of the traditional Indian wife and mother, who suffers her husband's and mother-in-law's constant berating silently (Ninan, 1995:129).

Singhal and Rogers (1999:89-90) provided a table (see Appendix A) to show the degree of parasocial interaction indicated in letters received from *Hum Log* viewers. The viewers felt that they knew the television characters even though they had never met them. Thirty-nine per cent reported talking to their favourite characters while watching them.

Apart from the estimated 200,000 letters received by Doordarshan in response to *Hum Log*, many fan letters were mailed directly to the private homes of the actors and actresses in the serial. Audience involvement with some of the *Hum Log* characters actually caused the scriptwriter to change the script. On one occasion, an outpouring of audience displeasure over the planned marriage of two characters was so great that the scriptwriter broke off their engagement on the screen. Furthermore, many young Indian women went to the home of the actress who played Badki in the serial to tell her she needed to resolve her indecisiveness and marry her boyfriend. When the two were finally united in matrimony on the programme people throughout India sent telegrams and cards of congratulations to the couple. And they closed their businesses early to celebrate the marriage.

One of the items listed by Singhal and Rogers (1999:89-90) in their table to show the degree of parasocial interaction concerns the role of Ashok Kumar (who died in December 2001). Viewers not only found him a positive role model but looked to him for guidance, and he was known as 'Dadamoni' – respectable grandfather. As Singhal and Rogers comment:

> Learning from elders is a cherished Indian value, and father figure Kumar doled out words of wisdom in his eulogies in a form of meta-communication, that is, communication about communication. Ashok Kumar's popularity, credibility, and friendliness, coupled with his words of wisdom, added to *Hum Log's* audience popularity and to its educational effects. (1999:86)

The final theoretical framework applied by Sabido was MacLean's Triune Brain Theory. This theory suggests that humans process messages in three brain centres: the neo-cortex (representing intelligence), the visceral (representing emotions) and the reptilian (representing urges such as sex). According to Sabido, sports programming, contests and pornography elicit reptilian-type responses. Soap operas typically elicit visceral-type emotional responses. News and political analysis elicit neo-cortexial intellectual responses. Sabido's technique was to use a soap opera's plot to trigger reptilian and visceral responses from the audience and to use epilogues in each episode to stimulate the viewers' neo-cortex (Singhal and Rogers, 1999:70).

Hum Log was the first major investment of the private sector in television software and heralded the arrival of commercially sponsored programmes on Doordarshan. It helped sell many consumer products by creating a market at national level for such goods, thereby giving advertisers the most cost-effective option. It also made the Mumbai film industry take to television production in a big way, which in turn brought talented people in to television from other media.

Hum Log was popular even after 156 episodes, but it had to be discontinued when it was at its highest level of popularity. Its storyline had come to a natural end-point, and the programme lost its political and bureaucratic patronage as key officials retired.

The astounding success of *Hum Log* spawned a number of soap operas, mostly women-orientated, in the next ten years. Some of these had little impact compared to *Hum Log. Rajani, Buniyaad* (Foundation), *Humraahi* (Fellow Traveller), *Udaan I and II, Yugantar, Adhikaar* (Power), *Pukaar* (The Call), *Aur Bhi Ham Raheim* (There are other ways), *Chauraha* (The Street Corner) were all telecast ten years after *Hum Log*. For example, *Nukkad* was presented by a bicycle repairer, a small tea-shop owner, a police constable, a friendly girl and later a teacher. In the words of Saksena

> It (Nukkad) projected the common man's actions and reactions, caused by different incidents taking place in the life of one or the other. (1996:113)

Another soap opera, *Kandaan* (1985), achieved some popularity because it was often referred to as the Indian equivalent of America's *Dynasty.* It portrayed the day-to-day wrangling, intrigues, conspiracies and rivalries in the life of high-class industrialists (Saksena, 1996:113). The soap opera *Yeh Jo Hai Zindagi* was more a sit-com serial than soap opera.

Humraahi

On 14 January, 1992, Doordarshan started telecasting the soap opera *Humraahi* – once a week for 52 half-hour episodes at prime time (9 pm). These episodes were the first part of what was hoped by the producers to be a five-year 260 episode plan. There was a six-month break between episodes 26 and 27, the first 26 shown in the first half of 1992, the second 26 episodes in the first half of 1993 (Population Communications International, PCI, 1994).

Humraahi was designed on the entertainment-education model introduced by Miguel Sabido and was produced by Roger Pereira, written by Manohar Shyam Joshi and directed by Kunwar Sinha. Training and technical assistance were provided by PCI (1994).

The main objectives were to promote and raise the status of women and encourage family planning and the adoption of the small family norm in India. In view of public attitudes related to the national family planning programme at the time, the 52 episodes deliberately did not deal extensively with family planning methods and services, but they did address such women's issues as age at marriage and age at first pregnancy.

> Central to the story line of this part of the serial was the death of an adolescent girl who was forced into marriage and early pregnancy rather than being allowed to pursue her dream of education and a career as an attorney. Her death in childbirth during episode 26 was a turning point in the drama, following which key characters pointed to the need for delayed age of marriage and the education of young girls. In the four Hindi-speaking cities where ratings were taken, *Humraahi* was (during 1992) the top-rated programme on the air during the times it was telecast. While nationwide, scientific studies of ratings are not carried out in India, estimates of the viewership of *Humraahi* have ranged from 100 million to 150 million viewers weekly on average. (PCI, 1994:1)

Funded with a grant of $76,700 from the Rockefeller Foundation, PCI undertook research on the effects of the televised version of the first 52 episodes of *Humraahi* on knowledge, attitudes and behaviour of the viewers, compared with non-viewers in the Hindi-speaking regions of India. However, given the long-standing traditions of Indian society regarding women's roles and family life, PCI recognised from the start 'that significant shifts in the direction of the adoption of pro-social attitudes and behaviours were unlikely to be realised in Indian society on a widespread basis after only 52 episodes of a serial drama no matter how powerfully it presented new role models to serve as norms for the modern Indian man and woman' (PCI, 1994: 2). Furthermore, 'the experience of Miguel Sabido indicates that the most rapid shifts in attitudes regarding an issue promoted systematically through a serial drama can be expected after 200 episodes – long enough for the audience to identify strongly with key identification characters, to follow their gradual change in attitudes and behaviours, and to adopt the new attitudes and/or behaviours on first a tentative basis and then a convinced basis themselves' (PCI,1994:2).

Nevertheless, the PCI conducted a quantitative evaluation of the project on the assumption that *Humraahi* had the potential to move viewers through some of the stages of change, from:

- not intending or contemplating adoption of the promoted value, to

- contemplation (weighing the pros and cons), to

- intention to adopt the new pro-social attitude and/or behaviour, to

- maintenance of the new attitude and/or behaviour.

The objectives of the study were to track attitudes regarding women's roles in society and to obtain perceptions of the serial and its cast from viewers. The present study draws heavily on the report of the PCI and permission has been obtained from them to use their materials extensively.

Methodology

The study involved conducting three one-hour interviews with an initial sample of 4000 people. Since each person was interviewed three times (except those who were unavailable for the second or third interview), certain questions, such as the demographic information about the respondent, were asked only once. Questions regarding viewership of *Humraahi* and identification with characters from *Humraahi* were asked only in the second and third surveys.

The first two surveys were conducted just before and just after episode 26 (in which the adolescent character, Angoori, dies in childbirth), while the third survey interview was conducted after the conclusion of episode 52. Survey Check I was conducted in June 1992, Survey Check II in August 1992, and Survey Check III from July to early September 1993.

The study took place in the two largest states of the Hindi belt: Uttar Pradesh and Madhya Pradesh. In each state four districts were selected on the basis of female literacy levels. It was assumed that the presence or absence of social inequality in general, and the status of women in particular, are strongly correlated with female literacy.

The sample interviewed for the study and its distribution was as follows:

	Uttar Pradesh	Madhya Pradesh	Total
Urban	791	799	1590
Rural	1227	1185	2412
Total	2018	1984	4002

(In the first survey, the entire sample of 4002 individuals was interviewed. In the second and third surveys, about 25 per cent of the original sample could not be located). The sample was spread across eight towns and 80 villages in the two states. Some of the relevant findings follow.

- Of the sample, 63 per cent of the respondents were illiterate and, as expected, literacy was lower among women (22 per cent) and in rural locations (33 per cent). (The study does not make clear whether this figure was an overall one or referred to women only).

- Interestingly, in a country with a reportedly high rate of unemployment, only six per cent of all those interviewed claimed to be unemployed.

- The respondents interviewed were married (85 per cent) or had been married (four per cent). As expected, the incidence of marriage appeared to be higher among women (93 per cent) and those living in rural areas (90 per cent), (presumably overall).

- The average age at which an individual married was seventeen. As many as 41 per cent of the married individuals claimed they had married when they were younger than fifteen (the lowest age at which individuals can legally marry in India is eighteen).

- Each married couple claimed to have given birth to what averaged at 3.6 children, three of whom were still alive. Asked how many children they planned to have overall, the average number of children a married couple desired to have was computed at 3.5.

Household demographics

Of the households interviewed 61 per cent were nuclear families (defined as parents living with their own children).

Full-time or part-time main earners involved 95 per cent of the households. Main earners generally appeared to be reasonably well educated, with 26 per cent of the households reporting that main earners were educated beyond secondary education (which in the Indian context means twelve or more years of formal education). Electricity was available in 61 per cent of the households

Family planning methods
Awareness

Forty two percent of women interviewed were unaware of any family planning methods. While, as expected, such ignorance was particularly high among women (49 per cent), illiterates (52 per cent) and rural dwellers (43 per cent), it was also significant that it was high among the young (age 15-25) and the unmarried: in both cases, 47-48 per cent did not know about any method. Most worrying was the 46+ age group, 53 per cent of whom knew nothing about methods of family planning. These are the parents and grandparents of children of marriageable age. Their ability and likelihood of persuading these children to adopt family planning methods is likely to be inadequate. The most widely used methods were sterilization and condoms.

Television viewing habits

Over 40 per cent of those who claimed to watch television said they did so every day of the week. On average, they watched for about 40 minutes on weekdays and longer on weekends. Irrespective of the day of the week, it was those living in urban areas, the better-educated and younger respondents who appeared to view television for longer periods. From the second survey to the third, *Humraahi* moved from second place to first place in popularity, with a claimed viewership of 33 per cent of all those who could name television programmes they had watched regularly in the last five to six months. *Humraahi* attracted more viewers among women, urban residents and the better educated.

Humraahi seems to have topped the polls in both the popularity and in conversation. Asked which television programme they had most discussed with friends and neighbours, eleven per cent mentioned *Humraahi* compared with three per cent for other programmes. Respondents were also asked if, as a result of watching such programmes, people would change their views. Over 50 per cent of the television viewers offered no opinion. However, in the case of those offering an opinion, the impression was that such television programmes could help in changing attitudes.

Viewership and impact

Detailed probing was carried out about the environment in which *Humraahi* was seen and the reactions to the programme and its cast.

*   The number of episodes seen: The modal number of episodes seen was 23 of the 52. The findings show that women, the better educated and urban residents not only watched *Humraahi* in larger numbers but also were more avid viewers, since they appear to have watched more episodes.

*   the overwhelming majority (87 per cent) of those who watched *Humraahi* claimed that they saw the programme in their homes (compared with the average television viewing habit, where only 54 per cent of viewers see television in their homes). A much higher proportion (nineteen per cent) of men than women (eight per cent) claimed to have watched *Humraahi,* which was broadcast late in the evening, outside the house.

Asked who in the household usually decided whether *Humraahi* should be viewed, the vast majority of *Humraahi* viewers claimed that the decision was made solely by them. However, the role of children and spouses (among adult respondents) also appeared to be quite significant.

Although *Humraahi* was viewed by the whole family, they seldom discussed it with family members. All viewers of *Humraahi* were asked to rate how interesting they found the programme on a three-point verbal scale. Fifty eight per cent rated it very interesting, 35 per cent somewhat interesting and five per cent not very interesting. When asked if they had learned anything from the soap opera, viewers who claimed to have learned a little or a lot cited issues of gender equality, education of women and the evils of early marriage. An overwhelming 73 per cent of the viewers found that the programme was a balanced blend of education and entertainment, while twelve per cent stated that *Humraahi* was more education than entertainment and eight per cent that it was more entertainment than education. Viewers of *Humraahi* were asked to state the issues covered in *Humraahi*. Seventy per cent of the viewers said that it covered 'status of women' and 73 per cent mentioned 'family harmony'.

Reactions were sought from *Humraahi* viewers about the various situations depicted in the soap opera. Respondents were asked to state how 'life like' the situations were. A number of social practices were perceived as being close to reality. Negative social situations that were perceived as being accurately portrayed were: teenage pregnancy resulting in death; daughter not being allowed to choose her partner; women wearing a veil in the presence of men; women who have not borne a son being harassed; preference of boys to girls.

Women and the illiterate tended to find most of the situations more realistic than the better-educated and urban residents. Certain situations evoked greater empathy among specified pockets, such as the practice of sending widows back to their parents' homes and that of women covering their forehead in the presence of men.

At the end of each episode of *Humraahi,* a popular film actress, Tanuja, presented a summary of the issues (her role was similar to that of Ashok Kumar in *Hum Log*). Fifty eight percent of the viewers of *Humraahi* agreed with her presentation while just eight per cent disagreed; a sizeable 34 per cent did not offer their opinion.

Changes in attitudes regarding social issues dealt with in *Humraahi*
Over 80 per cent of *Humraahi* viewers felt the programme would change the attitudes of people towards the role of women, the ideal marriage age for women, the ideal marriage age for men, the ideal age for first pregnancy, the use of family planning methods, and the ideal completed family size.

The table that follows shows the issues in the form of positive or negative statements with which the respondent (in the survey) was asked to express varying levels of agreement or disagreement. The scores in the right-hand column represent the extent to which the first 52 episodes of *Humraahi* attempted to promote adoption of positive social views regarding each issue. (It is important to note that) in the case of anti-social statements (for example, 'Girls should be married soon after they reach puberty'), a high score in the chart that follows indicates that great emphasis was placed on countering that attitude through the characters and story line of the soap opera. Most of the statements are worded in the form of a negative, anti-social opinion (PCI, 1994:40ff).

Emphasis on social values in *Humraahi*

Education   1–10

1. There is no need for higher education for girls since they   8
    are not going to use it

2. A highly educated woman drives away a prospective groom   4

3. A well educated man will fetch a higher dowry   3

4. It is more important to educate sons since they have to look   7
    after the parents in their old age

5. Education for women would help them to cope better with   8
    unforeseen calamities

6. Education spoils girls – they become arrogant and cause   6
    trouble for those around them

7. An educated girl naturally wants to marry an educated man,   5
    which means more dowry expenses

8. Educating a woman is like educating the whole family   4

9. Education helps a woman as much as a man in these modern   4
    days, even if the woman does not have to go to work

Gender bias   1–10

1. The birth of a girl is always a cause for anxiety   8

2. Performing household chores, like sweeping, cooking   6
    etc is not a man's work

3. Daughters should not be indulged   5

4. A girl is nothing but an expense   4

5. Female babies should be nursed for a shorter time than male   2
    babies

6. If there is a shortage of food/nutrition, men and boys should 2
    be better fed as they are the breadwinners of the family

7. A man has the right to beat his wife or daughter whatever   5
    the provocation

Marriage	1–10
1. Girls should be married soon after they reach puberty	8
2. Girls should be allowed to have a choice of who they want to marry	5
3. I don't believe in all this legal-age business; a woman should marry when the parents decide she should	5
4. Parents should pay a dowry for their daughters only if they genuinely want to	4
5. A woman should marry the man chosen by her father	3
6. It is best that a woman becomes pregnant soon after marriage so that there is no problem between her and her in-laws	5

Pregnancy/childbirth	1 – 10
1. If the first child is a girl, the mother should become pregnant again quickly so that she can have a boy	5
2. There is nothing wrong in having children in quick succession	4
3. If parents do not want a girl child, they should be free to terminate the pregnancy	8
4. The decision to bear a child should be made only by the husband; the wife should have no say	7
5. A woman should keep having children until she has a son	6
6. If the parents do not want a boy child, they should be free to terminate the pregnancy	NIL
7. Women who are pregnant should eat less so that they can have an easy delivery	5
8. There is no need for a pregnant woman to consult a doctor regularly; it is enough if she sees the doctor when she has some pain or bleeding	4

Child care   1–10

1. There is nothing wrong in giving boys special diet and medical   NIL
    care for longer than girls

2. The father knows what is best for the children. It is not right   2
    for the mother to interfere in the upbringing of the children

3. Both the mother and the father should have an equal say in   4
    deciding the future of their children

Woman's role   1–10

1. There is no need to spend scarce resources on a girl   6
    because she finally goes to her husband's family

2. A woman should not contradict a man, even if her views are   7
    different

3. A woman should strive to keep the men in her family   6
    comfortable, even if it is inconvenient for her

4. The responsibility for caring for a widow and her children is   7
    with the in-laws and not her own parents

5. A wife should not stop caring for her husband even if he   6
    is unfaithful

6. A daughter-in-law should be willing to sacrifice her happiness to   5
    keep her mother-in-law happy

7. A new bride should not be left alone with her husband;   2
    she will mislead her husband from his other family obligations

8. In a family it is the man's duty to be the breadwinner; the   5
    woman's job is to perform household chores

9. A woman should go to work only to supplement the   5
    family's income

10. A woman should be allowed to spend the money she earns in   3
    the way she wants to

11. A woman is not entitled to a share in the property of her   6
    parents since her share has been given as dowry

12. It is perfectly natural to prefer sons to daughters because they   7
    contribute to the family income and look after their parents in
    their old age

13. It is inauspicious to have a widow attending a wedding   4

14. Women should not mix freely when they are menstruating   NIL

15. A woman has as much right to live with her parents as has any man   5

16. It is not right for a woman to seek help from outside when she has difficulties with her in-laws   5

17. Parents have to be very careful of a girl's virtue after she reaches puberty, so they should not send her out unless accompanied by an older person   4

18. The main way for a woman to gain acceptance with her in-laws is by bearing a son   6

Effects of early marriage   1–10

1. A woman is not ready for marriage until she is 18 or so   8

2. Women cannot be expected to bear a child until they are old enough, say when they are 20 or so, because they are not mentally/physically prepared for it   7

3. A child born to a 15-or 16- year old mother will be weak and poorly brought up   7

Family planning related   1–10

1. The big families are the really happy ones   3

2. It is up to the husband to decide how large the family should be   2

3. The number of children I have is my fate; all the family planning cannot help   2

4. It is not manly for a man to be sterilised   NIL

5. A big family is more prosperous because there are more earning members   NIL

6. The purpose of marriage is to procreate   4

7. India will progress only if it can control its population   5

It is clear that the greatest emphases in *Humraahi's* first 52 episodes were on the role and status of women and girls, including the right to, and value, of higher education, the inappropriateness of son preference, the inappropriateness of marriage for girls soon after they reach puberty, the importance of delaying child bearing until a woman is mature and the importance of equality for wives with their husbands in making decisions about child bearing and other family matters. Many of these findings have been corroborated by other studies of *Humraahi*. For example, a qualitative survey carried out in the states of Maharashtra, Rajasthan and

Uttar Pradesh (quoted by PCI 1994:66), confirmed many of the findings of the PCI study.

Hum Log rode on the novelty of the soap opera format but by the time *Humraahi* was telecast, the audience was used to it. Both were spectacular successes based on the entertainment-education-communication strategy model and focusing on the use of family planning methods, the adoption of the small family norm and the raising of the status of women. A number of women-oriented narratives emerged. I discuss some of the more successful ones before examining the educational themes of the politics of family relationships, the role and status of women and the emergence of the New Indian Woman.

Comparatively speaking, there are few references to many of these soap operas in the literature. Consequently, I draw on the few references available, and in particular on Mankekar's (1999) illuminating study.

Rajani was a soap opera devoted to social criticism. The heroine, Rajani, is a middle class housewife who set out to expose social abuses. Produced in Mumbai and telecast over the network at noon on Sundays in 1985, the soap opera portrayed Rajani, 'fighting against corrupt bureaucrats, dishonest cabdrivers, brutal wife batterers and so on' (Mankekar, 1999:111). She questions oppressive practices and emerges redefining herself and the gender position within the structures of domination (Mitra, 1993:160-161).

Some serials telecast about the same time – for example, *Stri* and *Adhikar* (Rights) took the format of docu-dramas rather than the soap operas so far discussed. They were aimed explicitly at raising the status of women, discussed in Chapter 6. *Udaan* (Flight), telecast from 28 April to 21 July 1988, was highly successful and, according to the Indian Market Research Bureau (IMRB), during its run, '*Udaan* was rated as the second most popular serial in the primetime 9.00pm slot in the metros and the most popular one in the small towns' (quoted in Joseph and Sharma, 1994:282).

The narrative of *Udaan* hinges on a young girl, Kalyani, growing up in a family 'where injustice was done to her father and he could get no redress from the legal system'. Kalyani decided to enter the police force and the 'serial thereafter traced her story as she attained her goal' (Ninan, 1995:179). Mankekar (1999:137) has provided a comprehensive and illuminating account of this soap opera and here I draw substantially on her account.

The soap opera opened on the story of a feudal family in which the grand-father objects to his granddaughter, Kalyani, having the same educational opportunities as his grandson. Kalyani's father defied this decision and together with his wife and his children left the parental home. He set up home on a small piece of land given to him by his late mother and just when his hard work was paying off, the family was evicted in an illegal operation by a smuggler/criminal. Kalyani's father was determined to seek redress from the courts for the restitution of his property. His legal battles were unsuccessful and, to add insult to injury, he was beaten up by the smuggler's hoodlums. Kalyani decided to handle the matter herself; however, when the local police chief refuses to see her, she felt humiliated and powerless. She resolved to achieve power as a police officer, to sit on the other side of the table and, as Mankekar (1999:138) put it, have the power to help people who have been cheated of their rights.

The literature on the soap opera (Ninan, 1995; Mankekar 1999; Joseph and Sharma, 1994) refers to the aims, and objectives of Kavita Chaudhari who wrote, produced and directed *Udaan*. Quoting an interview with the Hindi newspaper, *Dainik Jagaran*, Mankekar states that Choudhry (another spelling for Chaudhari) claimed that *Udaan* was the story of a middle class woman's ability to rise above diversity...

> by dint of her persistence and hard work. But this, she insisted, was only half of the story. The other half was about Kalyani's struggles to be a conscientious police officer despite pressures from her colleagues to compromise her idealism. Chaudhry's ultimate objective was to show that a single idealistic individual cannot achieve much: what is required is collective struggle. She wanted to emphasise that it is the responsibility of all citizens to fight corruption. (1999:146)

Because of its policy (reversed in 1991) of allocating only thirteen episodes for a serial, Doordarshan incurred so much criticism from critics and viewers alike for refusing to grant an extension to *Udaan* that there was a sequel. *Udaan II* was telecast in 1991, in which Kalyani gets to the other side of the desk and acquires a policewoman's power. Disillusioned with the corruption of the police force and 'the ability of politicians and businessmen to bribe their way through the judicial system' (Mankekar, 1999:147), 'she finally turned to the non-government sector for help in fighting the injustice that the police force to which she belongs condones' (Ninan, 1995:181).

The late 1980s saw the highly successful and popular telecasting of the religious epics, *The Ramayana* and *The Mahabharata*. The impact of the telecasting of *Ramayan* and *Mahabharat* has been both dramatic and political and this is discussed here at some length.

Buniyaad (Foundation) was telecast in 1986-1987. It forms a bridge between the women-oriented narratives and the patriotic themes in Indian soap operas. Focusing on the tumultuous years following India's Partition with Pakistan in 1947, *Buniyaad* narrates the trials and tribulations of a Punjabi family striving to hold together. The bloodshed and massacres resulting from the Partition were so traumatic that it was not until 1975 that the Hindu filmmaker H.S.Sathu produced *Garam Hava* (Hot Winds) which relates the collective brutal violence against the Muslims during Partition. Just as the memorable performance of Balraj Sahni in *Garam Hava* left a lasting impression on the audience, so too did the struggles of the Punjabi family during the turbulent years after Partition, particularly as many of the characters had appeared previously in *Hum Log*. However, *Buniyaad* did not dwell on the brutality of the surrounding violence following Partition – in the words of Mankekar (1999:112) 'Partition is merely the backdrop for the saga of the survival of Lajoji's family'.

Buniyaad was perhaps the first major attempt by the Hindi film industry to enter television production. Ramesh Sippy, who had produced the highly successful film *Sholay* (Flames), was the producer and Manohar Shyam Joshi wrote the dialogue. According to Singhal and Rogers (1999:87) *Buniyaad* achieved higher ratings than *Hum Log*. Another soap opera which dealt with Partition was *Tamas* (Darkness). Like *Buniyaad,* the serial was made for Doordarshan by Govind Nihalan, a Bombay film maker, but who belonged to the Artistic or Parallel Cinema group. But, unlike *Buniyaad, Tamas* focuses on the conflictual Hindu – Muslim relationship and the violence it engenders. Mankekar (1999:291) makes the point that the author of the serial, Bisham Sahni, introduced the serial on the screen and claimed that his purpose in making *Tamas* was to expose the communal forces that caused Partition and are still active today. When the speech ended, the following words appeared on the screen

> Those who forget history are condemned to repeat it. (Mankekar, 1999:291)

The history of India is inextricably tied up with its two most celebrated epics *The Ramayana* and *The Mahabharata*. It is difficult to overstate the importance that these two epics have on the lives of Indians – indeed, they are one of the few powerful forces that have had a profound impact on the growth of the Indian cinema. Further as we put it in the book Indian Popular Cinema: a narrative of culture change

> The two epics are at the heart of classical Indian poetry, drama, art and sculpture, nourishing the imagination of various kinds of artists, and informing the consciousness of people. They have consequently had a profound impact on the development of Indian cinema and given it a unique Indian identity. (Gokulsing and Dissanayake, 1998:17)

The phenomenal success of the *Ramayan* and the *Mahabharat*[2] on television is due to a number of factors which have been comprehensively analysed by many writers (Mankekar, 1999; Mitra, 1993; Rajagopal, 2001 and others). Many of these factors are relevant to our understanding of the importance of the entertainment-education-communication strategy used by Doordarshan in its soap operas in the 1980s.

Part of the background to the televised Indian epics is provided in the introduction to this book: the decline of the Congress Party, and with it its avowed objective of secularism, the conflictual relationship between Hindus and Muslims aggravated by the rise of Hindu nationalism, and in particular the rise to political power by the BJP. Indeed, there was controversy surrounding the content of *Tamas*, mentioned above, which was attacked by Hindu organizations

> ...like BJP and the VHP who organised protest demonstrations against what they perceived as the sympathetic attitude shown towards the Muslims in the serial, while at the same time a writ petition was filed in Bombay High Court after two episodes were screened as 'everything shown in *Tamas* was against the Muslims, hence they were shown in a bad light'. (Gupta,1998:47).

The Bombay High Court ruled in favour of Doordarshan stating that: '*Tamas* is not entertainment. It is history' (Gupta, 1998:47).

THE EPIC SOAP OPERAS: RAMAYAN and MAHABHARAT

The Ramayana and *The Mahabharata*, combining as they do the art of storytelling with explicit social and moral commentary, have been an integral part of Indian childhood. Their picturisation entered 'the Indian psyche as a contemporary reference point in ways well beyond its maker's wildest expectation' (Ninan, 1995:8).

Was the serialised presentation of the two epics intended as part of a religious telecast or a cultural one? As Chatterji, a former Director General of AIR and at one time in charge of Doordarshan, has argued, Indian secularism meant that the state is equidistant from all religions — it supports them equally. 'Article 28 of the Constitution reads as follows: No religious instruction shall be provided by an institution wholly maintained out of state funds' (Chatterji ,1987:210).

AIR and Doordarshan do not broadcast religious programmes but due coverage is given to the public celebration of festivals of all communities. The media regularly broadcast devotional music from all religions and many cultural outputs have dominant religious motifs. Some of the religious festivals like *Durga Puja* in Bengal, *Onam* in Kerala and *Pongal* in Tamil Nadu have become community functions in which members from all religious groups participate.

However, Doordarshan's telecast in 1987 of *Ramayan* produced by Ramanand Sagar, a film producer in Mumbai, provoked extreme reactions. The programme became extremely popular not only in homes with television but even among those without. People travelled long distances to their friends' and relatives' homes just to see it. According to Lutgendorf (1995), the *Ramayan* serial was the most popular programme ever on Indian television with a rating in excess of 80 per cent (see Rajagopal, 2001:326) – and something more: an event, a phenomenon of such proportion that intellectuals and policy makers struggled to come to terms with its significance and importance. Never before had such a huge proportion of South Asia's population been united in a single activity; never before had a single message instantaneously reached so enormous an audience.

S.S. Gill, Secretary in the Ministry of Information and Broadcasting, took the decision to telecast this serial when Rajiv Gandhi was Prime Minister. His justification was that the '*Ramayana* is not only a great epic of Himalayan dimensions, it is also a repository of our social and moral values ... It has contemporary relevance for the human condition' (Gill, 1988).

Responses to the *Ramayan*, as Rajagopal (2001:137-138) has recorded, were 'wide-ranging and included observation on religion, culture, morals, science, government and nationalism'.

But along with all the excitement, the telecast was condemned by some as a cheap melodrama, 'filmy Kitsch'. At the same time, there were heated debates in the press and elsewhere about the folk and elite traditions, the marketing of religion, the suitability of telecasting such a programme on the government-owned network and the message of the *Ramayan* itself. Some critics were concerned about the state becoming the patron of a particular cultural stream (in this case the middle class and other aspirants to that status). For example, Romila Thapar warned that the popularity of the *Ramayan* might ruin the future of Ramila performances extensively staged in North India and in the process expunge diversities and present a single, homogenised version of the Rama story.

Fifteen years after its broadcast nothing of the kind had happened. Indeed, Lutgendorf (*op cit*) considered that the *Ramayan* was a cultural retelling in a new medium that affords distinctive possibilities to the story teller.

There was no doubt about the collective consciousness the soap opera fostered in the hearts of Hindus and this was a key symbolic backdrop 'against which the *Ramjanmabhumi* movement can be seen to have 'taken off' (Rajagopal, 2001:139). Rajogopal (2001) and Mankekar (1999) have comprehensively analysed the extraordinary series of events that followed the telecasting of the *Ramayan*. Politically, the consequences were incalculable. The national consciousness which emerged contributed to the consolidation of Hindu Nationalism. This was partly due to the homogenising of the *Ramayan* tradition by imposing a hegemonic north Indian, upper-caste narrative on its captive audience (Mankekar, 1999:171). The objective of the Hindu nationalists was to assert that India's strength as a nation is predicated on maintaining its 'inherent' cultural characteristics and that these in turn are based on claims to a heritage

> ...of deep spirituality (dependent, in turn, on physical discipline) and on the premise that ties between individuals must be subordinated to loyalty to the collectivity (the family, community and nation). (Mankekar, 1999:178)

Proclaiming that the nation of India had been weakened by Islamic influences, Westernisation and the policies of secularism, Hindu Nationalist parties such as the BJP and its allies whipped up religious feelings, fuelling the *Ramjanmabhumi* movement on a national scale. The political denouement of the movement was the destruction of the Babri Masjid in Ayodhya in December 1992 (Ninan, 1995:50), a cataclysmic event which has marked a dramatic turning point in India's political make up. Whether the telecasting of the *Ramayan* contributed directly to this state of affairs is difficult to determine. But there is no doubt that it contributed largely to it. And while there is much controversy as to whether Ayodhya was the actual birthplace of Ram, in the telecasting of the *Ramayan* Ayodhya as his birthplace was the essential backdrop to the story. The televised *Ramayan* and *Mahabharat* changed the nature of the popular culture genre in India.

What then was the contribution of the *Mahabharat* to the new scenario? Telecast immediately after the *Ramayan* and even overlapping with some of it, the ninety episodes of the *Mahabharat* ran from September 1988 to July 1990. It was telecast on Sundays and, according to Mitra (1993:90) and the *Times of India* 17 June 1990, broke all previous viewership ratings. It is estimated that nearly 92 per cent of Indian television viewers watched it – higher even than for the *Ramayan*. Its appeal was greater because whereas the *Ramayan* depicted a glorious Hindu past, glorified the ideal manhood of Lord Ram and was essentially based on Hindu religious practices, the *Mahabharat* was about India, an ideal India or *Bharat*.

Consequently, the televised *Mahabharat* cut across religious divides. Mankekar (1999:226) has described how non-Hindu viewers engaged with it. By combining religion and entertainment, dreams and desires and a glorious past, the *Mahabharat* 'helped to define a community, complete with values, a history and a future, and invited its audience to partake of its vision' (Gupta, 1998:48-49). This was all the more important since at the time of the telecast, India was going through turbulent times: the assassination of Indira Gandhi, tales of widespread corruption, a distinct feeling that the government had lost control over urban crime, spiralling inflation, sectarian politics and increasing communal tension.

What television did was to draw on existing cultural practices and rework them through the technology of television, aided by costumes, music and other components familiar to the Indian popular film industry.

The net effect of the telecasting of the *Ramayan* and the *Mahabharat* was to demonstrate the powerful role television could play in appealing to a nation facing modernisation. Admittedly, the appeal was primarily religious, and particularly to Hindus. And this was very conducive to *Hindutva* (see Glossary). Following the success of the two epics, mythological serials became a staple on Doordarshan. *The*

Ramayan and the *Mahabharat* were followed by such serials as *Shri Krishna* and *Jai Bajrangbali*. But given that Doordarshan was state television, Muslim viewers were treated to historical serials such as *Tipu Sultan* and Christian viewers to *Bible Ki Kahania* (The story of the Bible). It is noteworthy that *Shri Krishna* was aired on Doordarshan in 1996 and was dubbed in Tamil, Telugu, Malayalam and Bengali.

The rise of Hindu nationalism led to a number of Indian popular films based on nationalist and patriotic themes, such as *Roja* (1992); *Sardar* (1993); *Bombay* (1994); *The Making of the Mahatma* (1995); *Border* (1997); *Refugee* (1998); *Sarfoshi* (2000); and *Gadar* (2000). These spanned the nineties. *Param Veer Chakra* (*PVC*) telecast on Doordarshan from July to October 1990, also incorporates nationalistic and patriotic themes. There is little discussion of this serial in the literature; Mankekar's (1999) study is one of the few to deal with it in depth.

Mankekar's (1999) discussion of *PVC* does not make clear whether *PVC* is a soap opera along the lines discussed in the present study. *PVC* consisted of a series of narratives about the Indian army and air force soldiers awarded the *Param Veer Chakra*, the highest military decoration for service in combat. According to Mankekar

> Unlike soap operas based on melodrama, in which suspense revolves around psychological conflicts, the content and the trajectories of the emotional conflicts dramatized in *PVC* were predictable: heroes were torn between their love for their family and love for the nation; sexual passion was pitted against passion for the nation; and in all cases nationalist affect prevailed over the pull of other emotions... (1999:262)

Discourses of nationhood, national identity, communities and the politics of secularism

The secular nationalism which prevailed after the partition of India in 1947 until the 1970s has been challenged by a Hindu nationalism as expressed in the BJP's *Hindutva* doctrine – a clear-cut identity based on nationalism and patriotism. Culturally, the rise of Hindu nationalism coincides with the release of a number of films with nationalist and patriotic themes. As far as Doordarshan is concerned, the telecasting of several soap operas based on their entertainment-education strategy in the 1980s was aimed at improving the role and raising the status of women, considering the politics of family relationships and fostering a spirit of nationalism and patriotism. The politics of family relationships and the status of women are discussed in chapter 6. Here I examine this spirit of nationalism and patriotism.

A distinction is made between patriotism and nationalism. According to the Oxford Dictionary, patriotism is love of or zealous devotion to one's own country. The Collins Dictionary defines patriotism as devotion to one's country and concern for its defence. In popular perception, patriotism is associated with armed resistance to foreign invasion and rule. In one of the comparatively few discussions of the distinction between patriotism and nationalism, Billig (1997:55) quotes Connor's claim that nationalism and patriotism should not be confused through the careless use of language.

According to Connor, nationalism is an irrational, primordial force,

> an emotional attachment to one's people ... nationalism arises in ethnic groups ... Because nationalism is based upon a sense of the nation's ethnic unity, the national loyalties of 'immigrant' nations should not be described as nationalist. (1993:374)

Connor argues, therefore, that the loyalties engendered in the United States are not nationalist but 'patriotic':

> Despite the many advantages that the state has for politically socializing its citizens in patriotic values, patriotism – as evident from the multitude of separated movements pock marking the globe – cannot muster the level of emotional commitment that nationalism can. (Connor, 1993:387 quoted in Billig 1997:56)

Likewise, Snyder (1976:43) asserts that patriotism is 'defensive', being based upon a love of one's country, whereas nationalism 'takes on a quality of aggression that makes it one of the prime causes of war'. The problem is how to 'distinguish in practice these two allegedly very different states of mind'. In Billig's view

> ... some social scientists insist that patriotism and nationalism represent two very different states of mind. The distinction would be convincing if there were clear, unambiguous criteria, beyond an ideological requirement to distinguish 'us' from 'them'. (1997:55)

While the issue of patriotism has not been comprehensively addressed in Indian literature, nationalism has. For example, writers such as Kohli (1990); Oomen (1990); Chatterjee (1993); Varshney (1993); Kaviraj (1994) and Nandy (1997) have drawn our attention to the ambiguities of applying the terms nation and nationalism to India.

How do nations emerge and what holds them together? What accounts for the intensity and scope of national feelings? These are central questions for all nations, but for India they are now more crucial than ever before.

Taking the view that nationalism and patriotism are about devotion to one's country and concern for its fabric and defence, a useful framework for an understanding of nationalist and patriotic fervour as it affects the discursive and highly differentiated audience is Benedict Anderson's concept of 'Imagined Communities'. The phrase 'Imagined Community' signals a focus of loyalty, a source of identity and a sense of belonging to something bigger than oneself. According to Chakravarty (1996:11), Anderson's view of the 'profound legitimacy' of the nation rests on its diverse signifying power and the concept as experienced is associated with 'imagining' and 'creation'. Anderson sees the nation as an imagined community because, in the words of Smesler (1994:265), its members never know or even hear of more than a fraction of its members, yet they conceive of themselves as co-members of that overarching social unit.

Anderson maintains that the two forms of imagining, the novel and the newspaper, which first flowered in Europe in the eighteenth century, provided the technical means for 're-presenting the kind of imagined community that is the nation' (Anderson 1991:25). This emphasises the central role played by the image of a nation in acting a national reality

> In constructing an image of a nation, a large set of variables plays a role; religion, language, law, geographical isolation, economic considerations, bureaucratic decisions, colonial policies and the like. (Tamir, 1995:424)

Anderson's thesis is, however, not without problems. For example, his forcefully made point that the nation-state is a product of 'print capitalism' or the interaction between capitalism, print technology and the 'fatality of human linguistic diversity' (Smesler 1994:266) is not really applicable to the national integration issue which forms the basis of the 'imagined communities' in India.

There is no doubt that the telecast *Ramayan* and *Mahabharat* helped considerably in promoting an ideology of populism. The central ideology underpinning the two epics is one of preserving the existing social order and its privileged values. This ideology is furthered by the emphasis on Hindi and it is the combination of Hindi, the Hindu epics and the central role played by the television images of a nation's heritage derived from these two epics that allegedly contributed to the creation of a national reality.

How was this achieved? In what ways could these epic soap operas be labelled 'education-entertainment'? What problems arise when the state-controlled Doordarshan promotes 'education' arising from the telecasting of religious Hindu epics in a country that defines itself as secular?

It is within the historical and political contexts of the 1980s that the overwhelming effects of the telecasting of these two Hindu epics need to be understood. Religious disturbances between Hindus and Muslims, between Hindus and Sikhs over the separatist Khalistan movement in the Punjab, the closure of communication channels such as free speech, elections and a free press and other consequences stemming from the state of emergency of 1975-1977, gave some legitimacy to the telecasting of the Hindu epics. As Singh puts it

> What was unique about the TV serials was that millions of people watched the same show at the same time over a span of four years. As the epic-watching syndrome caught on, visitors and phone-calls were not welcome during the auspicious hour (Sunday 9.30 – 10.30am), petrol pumps shut down, and streets in metropolitan cities were deserted, while a nation sat before the TV set to watch the 'past' unfold ... (1995:81-82) (The actual telecast time was 9.00am to 10.00am)

While the audience were glued to their television sets, the educative functions of the epic soap operas, celebrating a golden age and cutting across barriers of age, class, caste and gender, were appropriated by Doordarshan and so reproduced that the central tale of India was repeated every Sunday, re-emphasising, in *Mahabharat*, its centrality in the lives of people. In the case of the *Ramayan,* Hindu nationalists rallied around the symbol of Lord Ram, now fixed in people's minds in a way that only television images could foster, and

> ...led the largest political campaign in post independent India... Television was the device that hinged these movements together, symbolising the new possibilities of politics, at once more inclusive and authoritarian ...The historical context was woven into and changed the character of Hindu nationalism (Rajagopal 2001:blurb)

Investigating how the televisual medium 'helps' re-imagine the nation and enable political mobilisation in new ways within the paradoxical conjecture of economic liberalisation and Hindu nationalism, Rajagopal has provided illuminating comments on the possible linkages between the televised Hindu epic soap opera, the *Ramayan,* and the mobilisation of the Hindu nationalists. He argues that the term 'fundamentalism' is more often used to describe movements in the Semitic religions

> where the sense of a corporate religion, based on one text and one prophet, delineates a 'foundation' that proponents appeal to. While Hinduism does not meet this criterion, the Hindu right has sought precisely to create a Semitic model, claiming that one text, the Bhagavad Gita and one god, Ram, express the quintessence of Hinduism. (1999: 76)

Referring to a number of sources, such as Colley (1992) and Bercovitch (1975), Rajagopal rightly states that

> The social and spiritual ties created by language could serve as an impalpable, quasi-religious means of resistance as well as a refuge, preserving the integrity and pride of the nation (even in defeat). The most durable and permanent basis of the nation thus lay not in states but within people, in their inner resolve to hold fast to the bonds that united them each to the other. (1999:54)

The *Ramayan* established the Hindi language medium across the whole country, as viewing numbers climbed from 40 million to 80 million viewers per week within a few months of its telecasting, according to audience research estimates compiled by market research companies. By its end the rating was in excess of 80 per cent. It is significant that the *Ramayan* belongs to a highly diverse narrative tradition drawing from Sanskrit as well as regional languages.

Following Luthra (1986) and Rajagopal (1999), religious broadcasts on fixed days of the week were ruled out and until the 1980s this was the working definition of secularism in government broadcasting, on radio as well as television. As Rajagopal observed

> The decision to air serialised mythological epics on television represented an important departure from previous policy in three respects. It meant that at a fixed time every week, there would be a religious broadcast. Further, the broadcast was to a national audience, and not just to the (local) audience of one station. Thirdly, by rendering it in a format meant for a general audience, religious programming was now being identified with culture in general, and not limited to particular festival days, or particular communities. (1999:60)

The assertion of moral values, of righteous conduct, of brotherly love, self sacrifice in a country then riddled with corruption, where betrayal of trust by political leaders was at the root of problems, was what endeared the viewers to the epic soap opera. It didn't matter whether relationships were presented in a syrupy, sentimentalised fashion and showed unquestioning submission to the orthodoxy of elders.

The telecasting of the *Mahabharata* so soon after the *Ramayan* did Doordarshan proud. In one sense the *Mahabharata* is the story of India, *Bharat* – indeed the epic is an allegory for the country. Unlike the *Ramayan*, whose primary character is a Hindu incarnation,[3] evoking reverence and religious devotion, the *Mahabharat* concentrated more on social and political issues. It was therefore more acceptable to a wider cross section of India's peoples. A survey conducted by *The Times of India* on 17 June 1990 showed that Muslim viewers found the show 'engrossing and educative'. Some were proud that a Muslim (the noted Urdu writer Rahi Masoom Raza) had written the script and that two of the major roles were played by Muslims. The survey also found that in some parts of the country Christians had shifted the timings of Sunday Mass, so that they could watch the serial. But the

> political implications of the telecasting of the Mahabharat were enormous. It was the division of the Kingdom – the lack of unity (which led) to the tragic war of Kurukshetra. In The Mahabharata Lord Krishna is pictured as the embodiment of goodness and divinity, the destroyer of evil. He is the spiritual guide of the Pandavas, whose advice to Arjun constitutes the Bhagavad Gita. In the epic soap opera, Krishna comes across as a shrewd politician – 'Krishna's wily politicking'(Singh,1995:82) – in helping the Pandavas towards their political ends.

Broadcasting these epics aimed to foster national integration and unity by articulating Hindu religious practices, using Hindi as the national language and imposing a hegemonic Hindu State. Thus, for example, 'each of the ninety-four episodes of the *Mahabharat* begins with the blowing of a conch-shell and the musical rendition of Sanskrit verses recited from the Bhagavad-Gita' (Singh, 1995:83).

Although mythological serials such as *Shri Krishna* continued to be telecast on Doordarshan in the 1990s, the formidable revenues which the prime time soap operas of the 1980s based on the entertainment-education communication strategy, including the two epic soap operas – the *Ramayan* and the *Mahabharat* – earned for Doordarshan dropped in the face of severe competition from the satellite invasion. Thus

> between 1984-85 and 1992-93 (Doordarshan's) annual advertising revenues rose from R60 (Crores) to R 360 (Crores). But in that year the impact of competition from foreign satellite channels began to make itself felt and the increase in revenues dropped off. Over the next two years the network's earnings rose by only R 40 crores ... (Ninan ,1995:147)

To meet the challenge Doordarshan used the Metro-entertainment channel started in 1993 to join the satellite channels in providing similar types of programmes. Furthermore, Doordarshan abandoned the successful format of its entertainment-education communication strategy such as *Hum Log*. It did so for a number of reasons.

Doordarshan transmitters carried both national and regional programmes and in the national programmes the time earmarked for entertainment programmes was just half an hour on weekdays and about two hours on Sunday mornings. This constraint led Doordarshan to allow only thirteen episodes of any serial accepted for telecast. Soap operas could not be completed within the time limit. Within the definition of entertainment, new genres like mythological and historical serials produced on elaborate sets with colourful costumes and plenty of music and dance, similar to Indian popular cinema, had become more popular than soap operas.

A committee appointed by the Ministry of Information and Broadcasting recommended that one hour in prime time be earmarked for entertainment programmes. Consequently Doordarshan made changes in its telecast schedule to provide one hour from January, 1 1993, but by that time Doordarshan had serious problems because of the new scheme of sponsored serials.

Doordarshan did introduce a daytime serial, *Shanti* in 1994. The first serial to be telecast five days a week, it was in the traditional mould of American serials whose main objective is to hook women viewers and keep them hooked on watching. Shanti, the heroine, was a woman journalist who wanted to avenge her mother's rapists. This serial became popular with viewers, who considered Shanti a role model. The telecast of *Shanti* was possible because of assured sponsorship from Procter and Gamble. Sponsorship of afternoon serials proved lucrative. Procter and Gamble's main competitor, Hindustan Levers Limited, promptly offered sponsorship to a second afternoon serial, *Swabhimann*, which was promoted as the sizzling saga of our supercharged times. The heroine of *Swabhimann* was the mistress of a dead industrialist and the script was written by Shobha De, a popular novelist. Similar soap operas followed. In 1997 Doordarshan set apart two hours on its national network for four afternoon soap operas, each half an hour long, and watching soap operas became a regular habit for women in rural and urban areas.

Soap Operas on Regional Channels of Doordarshan

Afternoon soap operas in Hindi were promptly joined by soap operas in the major regional languages. Calcutta *Kendra* of Doordarshan introduced a Bengali daytime serial *Janani* (Mother) which remained popular even after 230 episodes (nearly a year, with an episode every weekday) but had to be taken off the screen to accommodate a different producer. The story revolved around a mother who had to spend exactly three months of every year with each of her four sons, who lived in four different towns. One subtext of the story was the breakdown of the joint family system and the loss of primacy of the older generation (Gupta, 1998). *Janani* provided some stability as associated with traditional family structures. The soap explored threats to these structures; for example when one son has an extra-marital affair with a singer. The representation of *Janani* was idealistic, the dialogue dramatic and the situations emotional and sentimental.

Janani was followed by more popular soap operas in Bengali but success was not limited to Bengali. *Maaya Mriga* (mythical animal) in Kannada attracted enormous attention. It was watched in every home in the state even though it was telecast at the inconvenient time of 4.30pm. *Maaya Mriga* told the story of a middle class family belonging to a particular, easily identifiable community, but it appealed to people of all castes and creeds. The Kannada re-make of the Bengali *Janani* was also successful among Kannada viewers. Such soap operas were clearly popular with vast sections of the audience, irrespective of caste or language affiliations. Among regional language audiences the soap operas in the language of the region had greater appeal than those in Hindi, even though the Hindi programmes were of far superior quality.

Soap Operas on the Metro Channel

The Metro entertainment channel of Doordarshan which began in 1993 had introduced the new type of soap operas to viewers in non-cable homes, well before Doordarshan's national channel started its afternoon soap operas. One of the soap operas introduced on Metro was *Junoon* (Retribution). Revenge and retribution among business tycoons was its main theme. The husbands and lovers of glamorous women fought one another and these business tycoons were shown collaborating with the underworld (Ninan, 1995). *Junoon* was broadcast twice a week and attracted constantly high viewership for two years. Intriguingly it became a big hit in Chennai, a city that had always rejected programmes that came from Delhi. *Junoon*, originally produced in Hindi, was dubbed in Tamil and the Tamil audience was hooked on it.

Also on Metro was *Dard* (the disease). Radha is a young woman who married an older man due to circumstances beyond her control. She has an affair and gives birth to a son. Ninan reports that in a group discussion held in Delhi,

> the daring theme of a married woman's extra-marital involvement led to a lot of discussion and conjecture in the slums. The men were very critical of the protagonist, Radha, but everybody loved the ending, in which the widowed Radha opts for a life devoted to raising her son, rather than marriage to her lover. That virtuous and originally unrealistic resolution seemed to compensate for her earlier waywardness. (1995:185)

Metro channel ran many other soap operas. Among the most popular were *Imithan* (The Test), *Kanoon* (The Law) and *Aurat* (Woman). These new style programmes on Indian television could equally have been on Doordarshan or the satellite channels. The Indian audience was now in a global village exposed to soap operas of the kind viewed in western countries.

Notes

1. Only in a loose sense of the term can *PVC* be considered a soap opera – see further comments on p50.

2. *The Ramayana* and *The Mahabharata* refer to the sacred epic texts while *Ramayan* and *Mahabharat* refer to their serialization on Doordarshan. See also Appendices B and C.

3. According to Hindu beliefs, Krishna was an incarnation or avatar of the God Vishnu – hence a supreme manifestation of divinity.

CHAPTER 4

Soap operas on satellite television channels

As well as film-based programmes and game shows, ZeeTV also introduced serials. The sitcoms were of the 'filmy' variety and would have been rejected by Doordarshan producers as cheap and vulgar. Most were inspired by popular soap operas in the USA like *The Bold and the Beautiful* and *Santa Barbara*.

Tara (the name of the protagonist) was one of the early hits on ZeeTV. It was completely different from the women-oriented serials being telecast on Doordarshan. On Doordarshan, the women characters were keen to improve their lot and stand on their own feet, but they always observed societal norms. *Tara* was about the lives of four girls who left a North Indian town for Mumbai to realise their dreams (Page and Crawley 2001: 153). The story revolved around the cultural shocks they experienced as they moved from their conservative environment to a modern society. Tara, herself the daughter of divorced parents, is depicted as a strong-headed woman whose relationships became the subject of speculation in Indian households. She becomes involved with her boss, whose daughter Devyani never accepted Tara and much airtime dwelt on their strained relationship. Eventually the boss dies and Tara is ousted from the business (Page and Crawley 2001:153).

Tara proved shocking on several counts: a woman is raped; girls are portrayed living extremely promiscuous lives, smoking cigarettes and drinking alcohol. Again in the words of Page and Crawley

> ...*Tara* touched a chord with many young women who do migrate to the big cities in search of education and jobs and it played a role in making Cable TV popular in the smaller Indian towns. According to Vinta Nanda, the writer of the serial, it was specifically designed to spread Zee's appeal from the metros to the smaller towns. (2001:153)

By modelling itself on the sexual openness of American soap operas and by offering new role models for Indian audiences (Page and Crawley 2001:153), *Tara* broke the mould of previous Indian soap operas. It changed the contours of Indian television. Indeed, as the *Hindustan Times* (26/12/1999) put it 'If there is one show that makes Zee it is *Tara...*'

Another popular soap opera on ZeeTV was *Hasratein* (Yearnings). Savitri, the lead character is a beautiful young woman brought up by a strict aunt. She is married to a jealous man who resents her for furthering her career. Savitri falls in love with her boss and has a daughter by him. The boss, Krishnakant Trivedi, leaves his wife and the soap opera focused on Savitri's efforts to balance her love for her boss and for her own daughter. The director of *Hansratein*, Ajay Sharma said in an interview that the serial sought to 'explode the life of hypocrisy and double standards which enabled a man to have extra-marital affairs but made it unthinkable for his wife' (Page and Crawley 2001:153).

Like *Tara, Hasratein* was also controversial in many ways. The heroine's uncle was shown lusting after her more and more and even going as far as to visit her bedroom at night. Ninan (1995) refers to women in a media workshop protesting that situations such as shown in these serials would give men ideas but that they fail to suggest that intra-family rape was punishable by law. In discussion groups in Bangladesh, *Hasratein* was criticised for justifying adultery. In Maharashtra there was a feeling that this serial, which was based on a good Marathi novel, leaned towards vulgarity.

In 1996, Star Plus, originally an English language channel of Star television, became a bilingual channel and tried to challenge the supremacy of ZeeTV, investing hugely in software. The new package of Star Plus ran two soap operas. The first was *Saans* (the Life Breath), described by its makers N G Productions as 'the life breath of every Indian woman as it depicts her character, strength, virtue and steadfastness'. Nina Gupta was the producer, and also played Priya who has a pivotal role in the soap opera. She has a happy family, a loving husband, Gautam, a beautiful house and two children but this happiness is compromised when Gautam has an affair with Manisha. Priya tries very hard to win back Gautam, not for her sake but for the sake of her children. Priya starts an affair with a school teacher but refuses to marry him, again for the sake of her children. *Saans* became extremely popular among the educated and well-off women. But like most soap operas, it meandered on for over four years (it was still running on Star Plus in early 2000), then went unceremoniously off air.

Kora Kaagaz (Blank Sheet) was produced by Asha Parekh, a well-known film star of the 1960s and 1970s. It featured Renuka Sahani, who had acquired the permanent image of a 'good woman' on both large and small screen. The protagonist Pooja has the misfortune to lose her husband, Mahesh, on her wedding night. Mahesh had an affair with another girl and, after the marriage with Pooja, walks out of the house to live with his girl friend. In her new home, Pooja becomes the dutiful daughter-in-law, though her husband is not there. Ravi, Mahesh's younger brother, has respect for his *bhabhi* (sister-in-law) and gradually this respect turns to love. With various twists and turns, even after four years and 200 episodes Pooja and Ravi were still trying to get married in October 2001.

Recently, however, ZeeTV has been telecasting two highly successful soap operas – *Amanat* (Sacred trust) and *Aashirwaad* (Blessing) and we now turn to these as case studies of soap operas on satellite television.

Amanat and *Aashirwaad*

Amanat has for a long time headed the popularity rating of ZeeTV in a number of cities. As the *Hindustan Times*, a Delhi daily, announced

> No one had any inkling, except maybe director Sanjiv Bhattacharya, now no more, that his syrupy story of Lala Lahori Ram, who has more daughters than he can count, and whose sole obsession is to marry them off, would be such a thumping success. Dubbed the *Hum Aapke Hain Kaun!* (one of the most successful Hindi feature films of the 1990s which is supposed to have brought the family audiences back to the theatre) of TV, the serial's been Zee's pro-verbial golden goose (the channel had to create a special 'platinum advertis-ing band' for it), and it only proves that Indians love arranging marriages.

On a more serious note, *Amanat* unfolds the story of the valiant fight of a father who has to look after seven daughters and two unmarried sisters. The Hindi word *Amanat* does not have an exact equivalent in English but conveys that a daughter is a 'sacred trust' to be kept with great care till she is given to her husband and his parents. *Amanat* is a lofty concept essentially of the Hindi-speaking population of North India and Punjab.

The main character of the serial is Lala Lahori Ram, a businessman who has lost his wife and is left with seven daughters. He also has to take care of his two un-married sisters. He is a firm believer in the concept of *Amanat* and also expects that his sisters and daughters will adhere to the values he cherishes. Lahori Ram has a close friend Ahmad, who is Ahmad *Chacha* (Uncle Ahmad) to all the girls. Lahori Ram and Ahmad share all the joys and sorrows the two families experience as the story unfolds.

In the episodes telecast during the survey period, the eldest daughter, Santosh, is married and her marriage is not a success as her husband had wanted to marry Santosh's younger sister Amita. But her father-in-law fully backed her to the extent of entrusting the maintenance of all the business interests of the family to her. Santosh strongly believed in the concept of the inviolability of marriage – she felt that marriage is not just a contract but a commitment for life.

The second daughter, Amita, had loved another boy and against all odds managed to marry him. The twists and turns in the life of these two girls kept the storyline moving for about a year in the survey period of 2000.

Aashirwaad is the title of the other soap opera under study. The word *Aashirwaad* in Hindi and many other Indian languages means blessing and is of Sanskrit origin. When Indians meet their elders, they are supposed to greet them by offering *Namaskar* (obeisance), sometimes touching their feet and the elders in turn offer *Aashirwaad* (blessing) wishing prosperity to the younger by touching their head. This word appears to have a high emotional appeal, as a number of Indian feature films of the same title have been produced in Hindi and other regional languages and most have been highly successful.

The story of *Aashirwaad* spans three families and relates the complex interrelationship among two generations of these families. The first family is a traditional one, where the daughter has to obey her parents and has little freedom to act independently. There is little communication within the family and she has few opportunities to express her feelings. In striking contrast, the daughter in the second family has unfettered freedom and communicates freely with her father. He has lost his wife and has to depend on his daughter for many things. A third family is featured, which generally lives in a foreign country and is on vacation in India and the daughter of this family is not raised according to Indian traditions. She dresses in Western style and interacts freely with men, hugging and kissing them with abandon. All three families enjoy affluent lifestyles.

During the survey period, the storyline focused on the inter-relationship between the 'traditional' family and the visiting 'foreign' family. The father in the traditional family finds it difficult to accept the behaviour of the girl who is staying as a guest. He is particularly concerned about her relationship with his younger son. At that stage in the story he had some temporary financial difficulties and hoped for financial help from his friend from abroad. While he needed the money he feared that it might mean that he would have to compromise his values.

Objectives of the study

The case study aimed to explore the nature of the soap operas *Amanat* and *Aashirwaad* and their impact on Indian audiences. The main objectives of the study were:

- to analyse the factors which attract a viewer's attention to a particular soap opera when there are so many to choose from

- to explore the extent to which viewers identify themselves with the characters in the soap opera

- to find out whether a symbiotic relationship exists between viewers and the characters in the soap operas and if so, how strong this is

- to understand the social interaction triggered by the soap opera in the family, in the workplace and elsewhere

- to ascertain how far the viewers of soap operas agree with the claims made about the efficacy of soap operas

- to understand how much viewers are in agreement with the many statements made in soap operas about the role of women

- to obtain the opinions of the viewers about the changing role of women and particularly their attitudes and lifestyles in the big cities

Study Design – a sample

It was decided to conduct the fieldwork for the study in two metropolitan cities— Delhi and Mumbai. In each city viewers of ZeeTV were identified and detailed interviews were conducted with 100 people who regularly watched at least one of the two selected soap operas. Since soap operas are popular with women, it was expected that the sample would have a larger percentage of women respondents. The fieldwork was carried out between December 1999 and March 2000.

The two soap operas selected were two of the most popular soaps on satellite television at the time. The more popular of the two – *Amanat* – had an average TRP (television rating point) of 6 in Mumbai and 4 in Delhi. A larger percentage of homes in Mumbai than Delhi have access to ZeeTV and TRPs in Mumbai for satellite channels are generally higher there. TRP is the most popular television audience measurement of a programme and it varies from day to day. TRP is the weighted average of the percentage of the television audience that has watched a particular programme. This weighted average is taken for each minute of the duration of the programme and accordingly TRP gives the percentage of viewers who have watched the programme on a particular day. A TRP of 6 generally means that substantially more than six per cent of all people in TV homes in Mumbai have watched that episode. Though six percent may sound insignificant, this is not so, as ratings will always be low in a highly fragmented TV audience situation.

Selecting the respondents

Generally in field surveys different types of sampling methods are used for the selection of respondents. In quantitative studies adopting random sampling procedure is essential, as the sample is to represent the total population if valid estimates are to be made. However, in qualitative studies such procedures have much 'wastage'. To illustrate: if a random sample of 100 was taken among the sampled persons to get reactions on *Amanat* in Mumbai about 90 would not have watched it at all and interviewing those 90 would be a waste of effort.

Consequently, qualitative surveys use other methods of sampling. Snowball sampling is one popular technique and is often used to obtain a sample of people who are unlikely to feature in a random sample. Mytton explained the meaning of Snowball sampling and why it is needed:

> Snowball sampling derives its name from the way a ball of snow becomes bigger and bigger as you roll it. In snowball sampling you ask people with whom you make contact to suggest others they may know in the same category. It is not a method that is often used in quantitative work but it is more often used in obtaining respondents in qualitative research. (1999:32)

The procedure used in the present study was first to identify a number of localities generally inhabited by upper and upper-middle class people and select through enquiries some people in these localities who watched *Amanat* and *Aashirwaad*. With their help people who watched the soaps were contacted. But only one person was interviewed in any single household even if more than one watched them.

Using this procedure 100 people were interviewed in Mumbai and 98 in Delhi. The sample composition in terms of age, marital status, and educational attainment and occupation of the respondents and also the characteristics of the family they belonged to are given in the table opposite.

The socio-economic status to which the family of the respondent belongs is based on the education and occupation of the principal wage earner of the family. This system of classification has the advantage of getting around the measurement of income, a source of constant error due to consistent under reporting of income in India (see Appendix D for the percentage distribution of households by socio-economic status in cities).

Findings

Until the early 1980s Doordarshan, as we have seen, held sway among the viewers. There was not much choice or competition in programmes and televised drama in particular. But with the advent of transnational channels a large number of soap operas have come onstream, until it has become difficult to keep track of all the soap operas telecast on the different channels. Though there are many general entertainment channels in Hindi, some of these channels have become favoured for their soap operas. The avidly watched channels for this genre in 1999-2000 were Zee, Sony and Star Plus. The National and Metro channels of Doordarshan also had their share of soap opera audiences.

Table: Sample Composition

Respondents		Their Family	
City		**Type of Family**	
Delhi	98 (49)	Nuclear	141 (71)
Mumbai	100 (51)	Single	57 (29)
Marital Status		**Socio- economic class**	
Married	135 (68)	SEC-A	95 (48)
Single	63 (32)	SEC-B	88 (44)
		SEC-C	15 (8)
Occupation		**Occupation (Main wage earner)**	
Housewife	77 (39)	Professional	12 (6)
Regularly Employed	64 (32)	Executive	26 (13)
Part -time jobs	8 (4)	White collar job	98 (49)
Self-employed	14 (7)	Worker	6 (3)
Student	31 (16)	Business	45 (23)
Others	4 (2)	Others	11 (6)
Age (years)		**Type of TV receiver**	
15 – 25	56 (28)	Colour with remote	166 (84)
26 – 35	69 (35)	Colour without remote	22 (11)
36 – 45	40 (20)	Black and White	10 (5)
46 +	33 (17)		
Education			
Graduate +	158 (80)		
SSC/HSC	36 (18)		
Less	4 (2)		

(Figures in brackets are percentages of the total sample)

The popularity of these channels as carriers of soap operas cuts across all age groups and different socio-economic strata of the respondents though as elsewhere in the world, more women watch soap operas. Respondents in this study recalled several soap operas they had enjoyed watching in the recent past such as *Saans*, *Kora Kagaaz* on Star Plus, *Aahat* and *Henna* on Sony TV, *Amanat* and *Aashirwaad* on Zee TV.

Frequency of watching Amanat and Aashirwaad

Virtually all the respondents in the case study watched *Amanat*, 80 per cent of them regularly and eighteen per cent occasionally. *Aashirwad* attracted 66 per cent regular viewers and 25 per cent occasional viewers.

At the time of the study *Amanaat* had been on air for over three years and *Aashirwaad* for almost two. It seems that the appeal of both has decreased with time. Viewers apparently do not mind that the story is protracted over a long period though some media critics describe such protraction as torturing, with everything in the soap opera 'taking tantalisingly so long to happen'.

That watching soap opera becomes an addiction is confirmed by this study. Of the respondents, 68 per cent said that they had been watching *Amanat* for more than a year. Among the same respondents 53 per cent have been watching *Aashirwaad* for at least the last six months of the survey period.

The respondents were asked to recall how they had started watching these soap operas. Their answers are summarised below:

	Amanat	Aashirwaad
Usually watch all Zee TV soap operas at that hour	36	31
Some other member(s) of the family were watching it	20	21
Noticed it while surfing the channel and started watching it	11	17
Informed about it by friends/colleagues/relatives	25	19
Was attracted by the promotions of the programme	21	25
Read about it in newspapers/magazines	5	3

(Although the aim was to provide comparative data as percentages, multiple viewing has resulted in a marginal distortion of the percentages.)

It is significant that a sizeable number usually watched all ZeeTV soap operas at a specific hour, which indicates that there is some channel loyalty even in an age of so many competing channels.

Social interaction triggered by the soap operas

Soap operas often serve as a means of social interaction, providing a subject for discussion among family members, neighbours and at work. In such interactions the developments in the story in the previous episode are animatedly discussed and there will be speculation about what turn the story might take in the next episode or what course of action a particular character may choose in a given situation. About 80 per cent of the case study respondents said that that they discussed episodes of the two soap operas with others. The details of discussion are shown below:

	Amanat	*Aashirwaad*
In the family	59	62
With neighbours	43	41
At workplace	18	15

(*Some multiple viewing prevents percentage presentation.*)

Appreciation indices

Appreciation Index is one of the commonly used measures in Radio and Television audience research. Mytton explains the rationale behind the calculation of Appreciation Index as:

> ...Producers, Programme makers and Planners need to know not only who listens or watches and how many, but also what they think of the programme.... Audience size is a useful guide to overall performance of a channel or a programme on that channel. But it will never give you the whole story. We need also to take account of audience appreciation as a measure of a programme's achievement. ... Appreciation Indices can also be provided on specific opinions about a programme. (1999:91)

Viewers in the present case study were requested to indicate how far they appreciated the two soaps on the following aspects:

* main story
* structural development of the story-line
* unfolding the story in each episode
* performance of the actors
* overall production

The respondents were asked to rate the two soaps on each of these aspects on a five-point scale – Outstanding, Very Good, Good, Fair and Not good (or Poor). Appreciation indices have been computed giving the following weights:

Outstanding	4	Very good	3	Good	2
Fair	1	Not Good	0		

If all the respondents were to rate an aspect as 'Outstanding' the Index value would be 100 and if all were to rate that aspect as 'Not Good' the value would be zero, or in other words the range of the index is 0 to 100. An Appreciation Index is not an absolute measure but it gives an idea about the relative standing of different programmes and the strengths and weaknesses in different areas of a particular programme.

Both the soap operas scored high in the appreciation indices on the main story though *Aashirwaad* did better. In respect of development and the manner in which the story was unfolding *Amanat* scored low; obviously some viewers felt that it was a little slow. The histrionic talents of the actors in both the soap operas have also received high appreciation. In total impact also both scored high though here, too, *Aashirwaad* did better. Generally the Mumbai viewers were more lavish than the Delhi viewers in their appreciation of both the soaps. The Appreciation Indices on the different aspects for the two soap operas are shown below:

Appreciation Indices

	Amanat	Aashirwaad
Main story	64.8	70.3
Development	52.7	61.3
Unfolding the story	50.0	58.0
Acting	60.5	66.0
Total impact	58.3	63.8

As well as rating the various aspects of the two soaps, the selected viewers were also asked to give their critical comments on the two soap operas. Some of the viewers felt that the pace of the story was too slow. Some complained about the surfeit of advertisements that curtailed the duration of each episode, further slowing the pace. A typical comment was, 'Even if we miss one episode, we find that in the next episode the story has hardly moved'.

The respondents found the music of *Amanat*, especially its title theme, enchanting and felt that the musical score heightened the impact of the show.

Some of the respondents reported that certain incidents depicted and certain of the characters made a special impact on them. They particularly mentioned:

- the positive depiction of a close-knit Indian family
- the promotion of the understanding between the daughter-in-law and her parents-in-law in a joint family
- the need to bridge the generation gap and to avoid treating the wife or the daughter as inferior.

Some typical comments that were evoked by one or other of the case study soaps were:

- time and value systems have changed. Daughters should be consulted even in arranged marriages before entering into an alliance (*Amanat*)

- imposing one's decisions on the children is not a blessing but a curse (*Aashirwaad*)

- regimentation stunts growth and is not conducive to personality development (*Aashirwaad*)

- joint family is not an unmixed blessing. It has its drawbacks (*Amanat*)

- a girl should not compromise herself at any stage of her life (*both*)

- indian girls are taught to be tolerant, soft, right from the beginning so that they can easily adjust to a new environment after marriage (*Amanat*)

- the soap opera is helping the younger generation to develop love and affection for their parents (*Aashirwaad*)

- viewers are forced to reflect on what is right and what is wrong when they watch these soap operas (*both*).

Viewer identification

One of the main reasons for the popularity of the genre is the way viewers identify with the characters and incidents. The viewers love and occasionally hate certain characters. It is the soap operas whose characters have provoked such love/hate relationships in viewers that have greater longevity on television. The study explored the likes and dislikes viewers had of different characters to gain an insight into this identification.

The responses varied depending upon the social milieu, personality traits, family background, age and marital status of the respondents. In *Amanat* Lala Lahori Ram was a positive character, with his caring and protective attitude towards his daughters. His value system of looking upon each daughter as the '*amanat*' – the sacred trust – touched a sensitive chord in a large number of respondents. Santosh of *Amanat* was named another positive character for her unflappable temperament and exemplary sense of responsibility. Viewers were deeply touched by the friendship of Lahori Ram and Ahmed *Chacha*; many found Ahmed's genuine goodness and his affection for his friend's daughters inspiring.

In *Aashirwaad* it was Chaudhary who was the positive character, admired for his abiding faith in Indian traditions and particularly the Indian family system. But he had his detractors, especially among the younger generation, who considered him too orthodox, old fashioned and tyrannical. Arpana, the affectionate and self-effacing mother and wife, was also a loved and admired character, but the viewers despised the 'unscrupulous', 'the wily mother-in-law Preeti', and the 'rude and revengeful Geeta' of *Aashirwaad.*

The effects of television soap operas

How do viewers perceive televised soap operas? Do they consider that watching soap operas is only a way of passing time or do they think soap operas help in fighting social evils? Do they consider that there is too much emphasis on extra-marital relationships and conflicts in marriage? Several statements of this nature were read out to the respondents and they were requested on a five point scale to indicate to what extent they agreed or disagreed. Some of these statements dealt with what could be called the negative influences of televised soap operas while others spoke about the positive contribution of soap operas in advancing the status of women in Indian society.

The answers of the respondents on all the statements were tabulated on a computer. The data collected in this way was quite large and to bring this into manageable limits, Index values were calculated.

Index values

The rationale behind such Index values is now briefly explained. The data generated by tabulating the opinions of the respondents on two statements are shown below (for illustrative purposes only).

	Strongly agree	Agree	No Opinion	Disagree	Strongly disagree
Statement A	+33	+49	8	-8	-1
Statement B	+22	+40	10	-23	-4

Similar tabulation has been done for different variables such as education and the economic status of the respondents. As the figures above show, Statement A has received positive response from 82 per cent and negative response from 9 per cent. Statement B has received positive response from 62 per cent and negative response from 27 per cent. A larger number of respondents are 'strongly in agreement' with the first statement (33 per cent) than with the second statement (22 per cent). To measure the intensity of agreement an Index was calculated by assigning the following weights:

Strongly agree	+2
Agree	+1
No opinion	0
Disagree	-1
Strongly disagree	-2

If all the respondents were to strongly agree with a statement then the Index value of that statement would be +100, and if all the respondents were to strongly disagree with a statement, then the Index value of that statement would be -100. Note that the weights given are arbitrary and the Index serves only to summarise data to understand the relative levels of agreement or disagreement with various statements. The Index value will be 53 for statement A and 27 for statement B and it could be inferred that there is greater agreement on the first statement compared to the second (figures have been rounded off').

The level of agreement on the different statements represented by Index values is now discussed. Some people think that watching soap operas is just a way of passing time whereas others feel that soap operas help in a social cause. The respondents were requested to give their opinions on this matter and few supported the idea that watching soap operas is merely a way of passing time (Index value 23). There was far greater support for the notion that 'soap operas help in fighting social evils' (Index value 44).

Three statements concerning Women and Family were read out to the respondents and they were requested to indicate whether or not they agreed. A large number agreed that 'Soap operas have helped women in knowing about their rights' (Index value 44). Still more supported the view that 'Soap Operas have broadened women's views of the world – they can understand and appreciate problems of people they have never met' (Index value 59). On the other hand there was only moderate support for the idea that by providing common interests soap operas bring the family members together (Index value 28).

Respondents were requested to indicate whether or not they agreed about three statements concerning Marital Conflicts and Societal Norms as depicted in soap operas. The statement 'Many of the soap operas deal with adult themes and it becomes embarrassing to watch with young members of the family' had the support of a large number (Index value 52). The statement 'Soaps depict too much of extramarital relationships and conflicts in marriage' had the support of a moderate number (Index value 32). This was similar to the statement that 'Scenes of women smoking/drinking encourage some people to adopt similar behaviour' (Index value 28).

The respondents were asked to give their opinions on two issues concerning the impact of soap operas on the younger members of the family. The respondents in the case study did not subscribe to the view that soap operas give wrong messages to the young on love and marriage (Index value 6). On the other hand they supported the opinion 'Some of the soap operas help in bridging the generation gap as they present the view points of the other generation' (Index value 35).

The respondents in the younger age group totally rejected the idea that television soap operas give the wrong message to young people about love and marriage (Index value – 9 for the age group 15-25). This age group also expressed strong disagreement with the observation that scenes of women smoking and drinking encourage young people to imitate such behaviour (Index value 5 for the age group 15-25). On the other hand younger people had more faith in the soap operas' ability to help fight social evils (Index value 58 for the age group 15-25). Socio-economic class affected this response. Among the affluent, there was less faith about soap operas helping the fight against social evils (Index value 32 for SEC-A) than in the middle class (Index value 67 for SEC-C) and the upper middle strata (Index value 53 for SEC-B). Similarly, there were differences among the socio-economic classes with regard to the view that televised soap operas help women to know their own rights.

Perceptions of the status of women

One of the objectives was to understand how people perceive the role and status of women as depicted in the soaps. Again, statements were read out and respondents asked to indicate their level of agreement or disagreement on a five-point scale. Based on the responses index values on the level of agreement have been calculated on each of the statements asked and these are now discussed.

Televised soap operas have always advocated gender equality and the findings suggest that this message has reached the target audience. There was a high degree of agreement on three statements relating to gender equality: 'Women should be consulted in all major decisions', 'Sons and daughters should have equal rights to property' and 'A woman is capable of taking responsibility for the family when such a need arises'. All three statements scored highly – around 69 on the Index values. The negative statement related to the same subject: 'Money spent on a daughter's education would be a waste as she will always go to another family' was vehemently opposed (Index value of -78), which demonstrates consistency in their answers.

The traditional idea that women should always be more accommodating than their menfolk in the interests of the family still has a currency with respondents (Index value 57). In a way this could be an indication of the effects of the soap operas as they constantly reinforce this view. But the respondents did support the non-conventional viewpoint 'In extreme cases divorce will be better than long suffering' (Index value 47). A large number agreed with 'Most of the problems in a family arise because of men who do not show consideration for women and demand too much from them' (Index value 43).

A large number of respondents found the generalisation 'love marriages generally end in serious discord between the couples' to be too sweeping to be acceptable

(Index value -68). There was only moderate acceptance of the statement: 'there is nothing wrong if a daughter wants to marry a person of another caste' (Index value 34). Similarly opinion was divided on the statement: 'It is all right to oppose dowry but dowry has become a part of our life' (Index value 24). The statement 'Elders should always be trusted as they have the interests of the young in all their actions' did not get the whole-hearted approval of the respondents (Index value 23). Obviously the young people could not accept this view.

One of the criticisms about television soap operas is that they generally portray working women negatively. The respondents in the present study only partly endorsed the statement 'Women generally find difficulty in handling simultaneously the demands of a job and a family' (Index value 38). The statement 'Working women generally face discrimination at their workplaces' got only partial support (Index value 23). Similarly the statement 'One of the problems of working women is the envy of their women relatives' was not endorsed by many (Index value 23).

The changing roles of women in urban areas

In the last few years, there has been a sea change in the attitudes and lifestyles of women in metropolitan cities. Were these beneficial to the society, particularly women? What did our respondents think?

This case study sought the opinions of the viewers of soap operas on the changing roles of women, particularly the changes in the attitudes and lifestyles of women in big cities. Many of the changes were listed and the respondents were asked to indicate to what extent they considered these changes to be beneficial or otherwise to society. To obtain answers to this question, a five-point scale was used but the wordings on points on the scale were: Highly beneficial, beneficial, no opinion, not beneficial (or harmful), and not at all beneficial (or highly harmful). Based on the responses Index values have been calculated following the standard procedure and also vary from -100 to +100. Positive values indicate that the change has been viewed as beneficial and negative values suggest that they have been harmful.

Of the many listed changes, only two: 'Women no longer being confined to home but being engaged in gainful employment' and 'Greater interactions among all strata of society, overcoming the antipathy towards those in the lower rung of the social hierarchy' were considered beneficial to the society. The first was rated more beneficial (Index value 60) than the second (Index value 53). Some of those considered harmful to society, especially to women, were: 'Young people attending mixed parties till late hours' (Index value -55) and 'Couples deciding to break off their marriages' (Index value -46).

Other changes considered harmful to the society include: 'Young people giving less importance to religious rituals' (Index value -34) and 'Women often taking decisions against the wishes of their husbands/in-laws' (Index value -31). A smaller number considered retrograde developments like 'Young couples wanting to live independently, away from the parents/in-laws' (Index value -22) and 'some women deciding to remain single' (Index value -17). The respondents were by and large neutral to changes like 'Young girls mixing freely with boys of their age' (Index value -12) and 'Young women paying more attention to their make-up etc' (Index value +7).

Discussion of these findings is predicated upon methodological approaches and the next chapter discusses some of the theoretical and methodological issues under-pinning the analysis of soap operas.

Note

1. This, in tabulated form, is the method adopted for calculating the Index value for Statement A

	Strongly agree	Agree	No opinion	Disagree	Strongly disagree	Sum
Weights	+2	+1	0	-1	-2	
Percent	33	49	8	8	1	
Weight multiplied by percent	+66	+49	0	-8	-2	+105

Index value 105 divided by 200 equals 52.5

In a similar way the Index value for statement B will be 26.5

CHAPTER 5

Theoretical and methodological issues

Although the theories advocated by Sabido for the analysis of soap operas are mainly applicable to those based on the Entertainment-Education-Communication Strategy, some aspects of those theories can illuminate findings from soap operas designed primarily for entertainment, such as *Amanat* and *Aashirwaad*.

Carl Jung's (1970) theory of the collective unconscious, discussed on page 31, provides useful insights into understanding the appeal of *Amanat* and *Aashirwaad*. We have seen how viewers valued the archetypes: Lala Lahori Ram, Santosh and Ahmed of *Amanat* and Chaudhary and Arpana of *Aashirwaad*, and recognised the stereotype characters of Geeta and Gajendra of *Aashirwaad* who illustrated negative roles. This theory of the collective unconscious has particular resonance in India as Indians have cross-cutting, multiple identities. Weiner puts it like this:

> For much of this century Indian political passions have centered around the question of who we are, what our collective identities are, and how we establish collective self-esteem. (2001:207)

The archetypes mentioned above illustrate also one aspect of Bandura's (1977) social learning theory – viewers are enabled to share cognitively the behaviour of these archetypes. Bandura's main concern is about the harmful effects of the media on children. From Bandura's behaviourist position, children learn from media models what behaviour will be rewarded and what punished (McQuail, 2000:435).

Theories of the behavioural concerns about the effects of the media such as those formulated by Bandura (1977) and Berkowitz (1984) were common in the post war period but came under strong criticism, particularly for the authors' focus on stimulus-response models and their allegiance to experimental methodologies. As a number of critics (*inter alia* Winston, 1986; Lewis, 1991; Gauntlett, 1998) have pointed out

The fundamental flaw of effects research, such as the Bandura experiment, is that ontologically speaking it misunderstands the relationship between the media and society. (Ruddock 2001:38-39)

What is the relationship between the media and society? As Allen observes

a thorough reassessment of the manner in which traditional mass communications research in the United States has attempted to 'explain' the complex relationship between viewers and fictional programming is necessary. (1985:5)

Such reassessment has taken place periodically; for example, Klapper's summary of early research on the effects of mass media.

Klapper concluded that

Mass communication does not ordinarily serve as a necessary or sufficient cause of audience effects, but rather functions through a nexus of mediating factors (1960:8)

This approach is still useful and relevant. McQuail described how mass media research had oscillated between media power and media impotence, particularly since the advent of television. He summarised the various stages of mass media research, pointing out that 'for reasons which have been made clear, most direct questions about the 'power of the media' either make no sense or cannot be answered' (McQuail, 2000:486, quoting Nowak, 1997).

However, two pages on, McQuail states that mass media theory has 'opened up the endless complex subject of the nature of media culture'. He continues

Media theory has on the whole benefited from the work of cultural theorists who have colonized the once rather limited theory founded mainly upon psychology, sociology and politics. (2000:488)

Herein lies the basis for a stimulating discussion of the contributions of cultural theorists to our understanding of popular culture. It is important in relation to television, *the* popular cultural form of the late twentieth century. And soap operas are arguably the most popular genre on television worldwide.

There are comprehensive reviews of the emergence of Cultural Studies as a distinct field of academic inquiry and its contributions to popular culture (*inter alia* Hall, 1981; Storey, 1993; Turner, 1996; Strinati, 1995). Drawing upon this extensive literature and selecting issues which are relevant to our understanding of soap operas as popular culture, we find that culture is, as Williams says,

One of the two or three most complicated words in the English language... because it has now come to be used for important concepts in several distinct intellectual disciplines and in several distinct systems of thought. (1976:76-7)

The development of Cultural Studies as a distinct field of academic inquiry and its importance in Britain originated at the Centre for Contemporary Cultural Studies (CCCS) of the University of Birmingham in the 1950s. Raymond Williams and Richard Hoggart were instrumental in developing the CCCS, but it was Stuart Hall and his colleagues who established it as an 'institutionally significant moment' (Barker, 2000:6). Indeed, what became known as the Birmingham School flourished for nearly two decades from the early 1970s. Heavily influenced by Marxist ideas, it concentrated its work, as Graeme Turner (1996) has shown, on three main themes:

- textual studies of the mass media and the ways that these operate to reproduce hegemony and ideology

- ethnographic explorations of everyday life, especially those of subcultures

- studies of political ideologies such as those of Thatcherism and racist nationalism. (See Smith, 2001:155)

In the early stages of their critical exploration, Cultural Theorists used two related concepts to interrogate television as a popular culture medium: ideology and hegemony. Storey (1996:4) has explained how Hall, drawing on Gramsci's idea of hegemony and Althusser's concept of ideology, claims that the ideological messages of the media work towards creating a false image of reality. Hall developed a theory of articulation to explain 'the processes of ideological struggle'. Storey points out that

> Cultural texts and practices are multi accentual; that is, they can be articulated with different 'accents' by different people in different contents for different politics. Meaning is therefore a social production... A text or practice or event is not the issuing source of meaning, but a site where the articulation of meaning – variable meaning(s) – can take place... Thus the field of culture is for cultural studies a major site of ideological struggle, a terrain of 'incorporation' and 'resistance'. (1996:4)

The field of Cultural Studies has moved on to develop a multidisciplinary approach to culture, focused not only on working class youth and subcultures, but also more radical approaches such as feminism and semiotics, antiracist and gay liberation movements (see Bounds , 1999 for a brief but clear summary).

The dramatic impact of feminism on the analysis of soap operas is well documented too (Ang, 1985; Hobson, 1982; Radway, 1984; Geraghty, 1991; Modleski, 1982; Brown, 1994, for example). Feminism as an intellectual and political activity has a long history (Spender 1985), but of particular relevance to our study is the body of work from feminists since the 1970s. Focusing on the binary opposition between sex and gender, feminists have demonstrated how

> sex is a fundamental and irreducible axis of social organisation which, to date, has subordinated women to men whereas gender relations are thoroughly saturated with power relations. (Barker, 2000:24)

While much has been written about, for example, the exclusion of women from the public sphere (Long, 1991), gendered language and syntax (Cixous, 1987) and in ethics (Gilligan, 1982), it is only in recent years that the academic study of soap operas has become respectable. In the words of McQuail,

> most central to critical feminist analysis is probably the broad question (going beyond stereotypes) of how texts 'position' the female subject in narratives and textual interactions and in so doing contribute to a definition of femininity in collaboration with the 'reader'. (2000:310)

In dealing with the questions posed here by McQuail, an audience analysis with special reference to the Indian audience sheds light on whether or not Indian soap operas challenge gender stereotyping and have empowering effects for women.

Constructing the Audience

Like language, which changes over time through use, the concept of the audience has undergone dramatic transformation over the last fifty years. Recent studies of audiences (*inter alia* Abercrombie and Longhurst 1998; McQuail 1997; Nightingale 1996; Ruddock 2001) have charted this transformation of the audience from its early days as a mass of passive, atomistic individuals to a more sophisticated, participatory concept of an active audience. Abercrombie and Longhurst (1998:1-2) have argued for three different types of audience: simple, mass and diffused, to reflect the paradigmatic shifts in the construction of the audience from its early years to the present day. I believe, like Abercrombie and Longhurst (1998), that the interactions between these three audience types are important and it is useful to sketch the stages of the transformation of the concept of the audience and their implications for research.

It is customary to identify the following phases in this transformation:

- The earliest phase – the 1930s, associated with the Frankfurt School, theorised that owing to the breakdown of society into a collection of atomised individuals, people were very vulnerable, particularly to the forces of propaganda.

- This hypodermic needle model of media influence was challenged in the 1940s and 1950s by American researchers who posited a model whereby media messages were mediated by 'opinion leaders'.

- Until the 1960s the debate about the effects of the media was mainly about whether or not television had direct effects on its audience. The position was well summed up by Klapper (1960).

- The next phase of audience research from the 1960s to the 1980s is associated with the Uses and Gratifications approach, which shifted the kind of questions asked about the effects of television on its audience. The effects tradition looked at what television did to audiences; the Uses and Gratifications approach looked at what audiences did with television. As Abercrombie (1996:141-142) explained: 'the viewer in this scheme was treated as having certain needs, generated by a range of social processes which television satisfied'.

The Uses and Gratifications approach was very popular with the commercial media industry which was keen to promote the idea that the industry's aim was to meet the needs of its various customers.

A breakthrough occurred in the 1970s when Stuart Hall's influential paper 'Encoding and Decoding the TV message' (1973) laid the foundations for an alternative approach to the study of the communication process. Arguing that texts are 'polysemic' and that the text-reader relationship takes the form of a negotiation (Eldridge *et al* 1997:131), Hall's formulation shifted the study of the audience from a behaviouristic stimulus-response model based on a psychological conception of human personality to one based on a social theory of subjectivity and meaning construction. As Eldridge *et al* pertinently put it:

> Hall's argument is that the range of different interpretations are not free-floating or individual readings but are influenced by the social context...He is interested in 'inking in the boundaries of various interpretive communities', drawing up a 'cultural map' of the audience, and relating these to social and political processes. (1997:131)

This approach – Reception Studies – led to a number of significant studies, sociologically informed and in-depth empirical work that dealt with actual audiences in the 1980s and 1990s. Morley's (1980) 'Nationwide' study is probably the best example to confirm Hall's theory.

This seminal study is now seen as leading the first generation of Audience Reception research in media studies. However, focusing upon the production of meaning in the encoding and decoding formulation did not pay adequate attention to the functions of consumer activities. Consequently, the second generation of Audience Reception research moved away from the 'semiotic turn' of the first generation to an 'ethnographic turn' in which several important qualitative audience reception studies were undertaken. These include Ang (1985) and Hobson (1982).

There are now a number of different ways of looking at audience reception. These include:

- A shift from conventional politics to identity politics, particularly questions of gender

- More emphasis on the medium (Lull, 1980)

- Greater focus on television as a social resource for conversation

- Greater focus on the way in which television use reflects and reproduces (gendered) relations of power in family life.

More recently, some writers (*inter alia* Ang, 1989; Grossberg, 1988; and Radway, 1988) began to question and discuss the premises of the audience's ethnography. This third generation of audience reception calls for a thorough rethinking of the place of the media in everyday life, the concept of audience and along with that the place of media research itself in the whole picture. In particular, ordinary people do not just watch television without reflecting on the activity. Radway (1984), for example, has emphasised that instead of one particular circuit of producer, text and audience, it is people's daily lives that must be the point of departure and object of research (Alasuutari, 1999).

Carrying out empirical work in this situation – which Alasuutari (1999:6) calls a constructionist view – is problematic. Even more problematic is the relevance of audience studies research to the televised Indian soap operas within these various views of audience analysis.

Researching the Indian Audience

Mankekar's (1999) contribution is one of the very few with an ethnographic approach to the study of Indian soap operas that provides illuminating insights into the politics of the family, womanhood, community and the nation. However, Srinivas, in a short, illuminating article, is scathing in his criticisms. He finds her study

> ...does not offer much information to those who are familiar with the debates on Indian television... The findings of Mankekar's ethnographic work as well as their presentation are disappointing... (2001:120-121)

In particular, Srinivas takes exception to Mankekar's inability to argue how television provides information that justifies the pleasures of television, her construction of the family audience as an invention of television, thereby ignoring the crucial role played by the cinema in contributing to the family audience and the genre of devotional films. In all these media genres, the cinema laid the ground for the pre-televisual forms.

Also relevant are the Screen Theory developments in film theory which viewed the audience through a detailed examination of the structure of the text and an examination of how that text positions the reader (Eldridge *et al* 1997:127-128). Referring to the contributions of such writers as Stephen Heath, Laura Mulvey and Colin

MacCabe, Eldridge *et al* state that drawing on French film theory and Lacanian psychoanalysis, the Screen Theory writers argue

> how subjectivity does not simply exist as a static and unified entity but is created through language and culture... In particular, they (the screen theory writers) are interested in how the cinematic text confers subjectivity upon readers, sewing or 'suturing' them into the film's narrative through the production of subject position. (1997:128)

What traditional cinematic devices clearly do, according to the arguments advanced by the Screen Theory writers, is to position the spectators in such a way (particularly through camera angles, shot/reverse shots) that they are sucked into the film's ideology. The traditional Hollywood film is viewed as extremely powerful, making the spectator a prisoner of the text, seen as monolithic. This Dominant Text position can be countered by a Dominant Audience position which sees the text as polysemic, containing a number of possible meanings and therefore allowing a range of audience interpretations. Morley's (1980, 1989, 1992) path-breaking analyses of media studies, already mentioned, have shown how complex responses to the media can be (Abercrombie and Longhurst 1998:17). But what relevance do references to the cinema audience have to the discussion about the viewers of Indian soap operas?

Until the 1980s and particularly since the advent of satellite television in the 1990s, Indian cinema was India's most popular activity. Except for very brief notes in one or two studies of Indian soap operas, the role of the Indian popular cinema is barely acknowledged. Mankekar's (1999:73 note 35) brief note does refer to the ambivalent relationship between Bollywood and Doordarshan but suggests that this relationship is 'complex and warrants a separate investigation'.

Although I do not wish to engage in a separate investigation of this complex relationship, some aspects of it provide illuminating insights into the enormous popularity of Indian soap operas, since these have now replaced the cinema as India's foremost hegemonic popular culture. This relationship can be explored through a number of concepts/issues.

There is no doubt that an important aspect of the highly successful televised epics of the *Ramayan* and the *Mahabharat* derives from the long history of the genres of mythological and devotional films. As Gokulsing and Dissanayake observe about mythological films:

> Mythological films constitute a very important segment of Indian popular cinema. They have their roots in the ancient past in that they deal with characters and events taken from the distant past, very often as inscribed in the epics and scriptures... But they are not merely historical; they portray the interface between the past and the present. (1998:24-25)

The genre of devotional films includes *Sant Tukaram* (1936), *Sant Tulsidas* (1939), *Jai Santoshi Ma* (1975), and *Adi Shankaracharya* (1983). What these films do is to highlight religious symbols, concepts and images which then play a key role in framing the narrative and investing it with meaning.

An essential ingredient of the appeal of the Indian popular cinema, and particularly the televised epics, is the concept of spectacle. According to the Oxford Dictionary, spectacle is a public show, a visually striking performance. But as far as the Indian popular cinema is concerned and also the televised epics of *Ramayan* and *Mahabharat*, spectacle also means exposing, seeing and watching (Hayward, 1996:286). Indeed, with the increasing importance of new technology and the increasing transformation of India from a traditional, pre-modern country to one with a significant position in a globalised world, the whole world has become an object of spectacle, a set of performances.

How is the Indian viewer situated within this globalised world? A world where on the one hand, the state-controlled television (Doordarshan) tried to advocate social change through a number of commercially-sponsored soap operas in which the traditional values of Indian life draw upon invocations of a glorious heritage and elements of myth and, on the other hand, depict a new India and the emergence of a new Indian woman, with all this implies for the health, welfare and stability of the traditional Indian family? One way of understanding this re-positioning of the nation of India is to look closely at the relevance of the two concepts of globalisation and media imperialism, as applied to Indian television.

Globalisation – The Indian experience

We saw that Doordarshan was forced to rethink its strategy and policies in the 1990s in order to respond to the increasing competition from cable and satellite channels like ZeeTV, Star and Sony. Within a short time, there has been an exponential growth in the number of television channels. The position in 2001 was, according to Cable Operators Federation of India, as follows:

Television homes	70 million
Cable and Satellite homes	30 million
Viewers	400 million
	(India's population 1 billion)
Cable operators	70,000
Cable revenue	Rs 36 billion

(Sonwalkar, 2001:517)

Coupled with India's new economic policies of liberalisation and its rapidly expanding middle class (variously estimated to be between 200 and 250 million) with aspirations to a western life style, the significant economic and cultural changes taking place in India are part of the globalisation process. Globalisation, as Lal (2000:35) has stated, '...is the process whereby national commodity and capital (but currently, not labor) markets are being internationally integrated'.

Although there are different views of the upsurge of globalisation in various parts of the world, it is generally agreed that globalisation has ushered in a new era. Economic reforms are being forced upon nations by multinational companies driven by market forces and technological developments. Consequently, much attention has been paid to the econocentric aspects of globalisation (see inter alia Bauman, 1998; Hirst and Thompson, 1996; Giddens, 1990; Robertson, 1992 for further discussion) but comparative little to the cultural aspects. Tomlinson has tried to redress this inattention by providing some useful insights into the social 'production of existentially significant meaning; culture in a globalised context – like politics and economics – is shaped by a complex connectivity...' (1999: Chapter 1). This connectivity 'involves the integration of individual and collective actions into the way institutions actually work' (1999:24).

Globalisation has transformed India in two decades. In her book *India – Globalisation and Social Change*, Shurmer-Smith (2000) examined the political and social changes taking place in India as a result of market liberalisation and integration into the world economy. She focused on the modernising forces at work in India through an analysis of four major themes: caste, class, religion and gender. She demonstrates how the Hindu Right has tried to forge a corporate Hindu identity by 'othering' India's minorities, by bringing the lower castes under the wing of the upper class elites, by targeting middle class women because the Right resents their new images as presented by the satellite channels and by condemning the breakdown of the institutions of marriage and extended families by the forces of globalisation.

We have seen how soap operas on Doordarshan since the 1980s and on satellite channels since the 1990s provided examples of both traditional and modern images of India during a state of transition. To what extent are the modern images of India and its citizens a result of the cultural aspects of globalisation?

A number of writers (see for example Schiller, 1976; Tunstall, 1977; Katz and Wedell, 1978; Mattelart, 1979; Lee 1981) have suggested the media imperialism approach – a one-way flow of cultural production from the developed to the developing world as having a significant impact on the role of television in many countries. According to this approach

> a small group of western countries not only controlled the international media trade, but used it to transmit their particular cultural and economic values, particularly individualism and consumerism, to large numbers of developing nations around the world. (Chadha and Kavoori, 2000:416)

In recent years the media imperialism approach has come under increasing criticism since it fails to take account of the fact that countries such as Brazil and India are both major producers and also global exporters of audio visual materials. Cultural imperialism is an equally fashionable term preferred by Neo Marxists since they find the term media imperialism too constricting. Writers like Schiller (1976) and Mattelart (1979) have written about the perceived cultural and communication hegemony of the west, and in particular of the United States. This too has come under criticism by writers such as Tomlinson (1991) and Schlesinger (1991) who have critiqued the implications of the term cultural imperialism, arguing that countries (like India) do not necessarily act as cultural sponges. Central to any argument about cultural imperialism is transnational capitalism. Tomlinson (1991), dissecting the constituent parts of the term 'cultural imperialism', finds that in one sense, particularly with the emphasis on the word imperialism, the implications are that the west and transnational capitalism are the enemies of the cultural autonomy of other countries, particularly developing ones.

There is some substance in this view. For example, an advertising company survey conducted in 1996 asked people in nineteen different countries about the television programmes they preferred. Over 41 percent of the 20,000 respondents considered US programmes excellent or very good, nearly twice the level of the nearest rival (Tomkins, 1996, quoted in Lewis, 2002:347). Like food, soap operas travel well in many countries, whatever their origins. For example, more than 400 million people worldwide, including in countries such as Russia, Tunisia, Zimbabwe and Switzerland, regularly watch TV soap operas that originate in Spanish-language nations (Lull, 1995:145 – quoted in Lewis, 2002:355).

These views reinforce arguments made by Tunstall (1977) and others that the strength of world capitalism is directly related to its ability to sell not merely goods but also ideas and more generally ideologies that sustain our levels of consumption. The growth of consumerism – a culture geared to the promotion, sale and acquisition of consumer goods – is heavily dependent on the growth of transnational media dominated by Sony, Sky TV, CBS and so on. While a common western-centric culture dynamic may prevail, we agree with Smith (1992) that 'globalisation has instead led people in many countries to renew their loyalty to the local, to tradition, ethnicity and national culture'.

Consequently, in the next chapter we provide some analysis of the role and impact of televised Indian soap operas along the lines indicated by Smith. More concretely, we deal with family relationships, fertility control and the emergence of the new Indian woman as reflected in the televised Indian soap operas.

CHAPTER 6

The politics of family relationships, birth control and women-oriented soap operas

An important aspect of the politics of family relationships is birth control. Initially, one of the main aims of *Hum Log* was, according to Singhal and Rogers (1999), to provide information and advice on family planning. But the pro-social messages about family planning did not have a significant effect on viewer's family beliefs, for reasons described in chapter 3. We also know that not only did script writer Manohar Shyam Joshi tone down the family planning messages but he also brought in issues dealing with family harmony, the status of women and national integration. A content analysis carried out by Brown (1990) showed that women's concerns represented a large percentage of the pro-social content in the series.

A number of writers, particularly women (see for example Chatterjee and Riley, 2001; Krishnaraj, Sudarshan, and Shariff, 1998; Srinivasan, 1995) have drawn our attention to how the 'linking of individual and family reproductive behaviour to national welfare and the promotion of modernity as embodied practice is itself an inherently modern project' (Chatterjee and Riley, 2001:811) and is part of the hegemonic western conception of the modern.

An essential element of the modernisation process was the control of what was seen as an excessively high birth rate and population growth. There is no doubt that the poor and lower caste working women were targeted (Chatterjee and Riley, 2001). Women activists have taken issue with the government about their policy of female contraception, arguing that the government was fostering gender inequalities. While the slogan *Chhota Pariwar: Sukh Ka Adhar* (small family, happy family) makes sense to both traditionalists and modernisers in India, the methods advocated don't. For example, Mahatma Gandhi (and his followers) associated birth control with immorality and advocated sexual restraint to reduce family size. Moreover, contraception is never linked to unrestrained sexuality and seldom to non-familial roles. The forward-thinking woman is identified with home and family in a way not often seen in the West. The gap between Western and Indian versions of modernity is also apparent in the conceptualisation of families as conjugal units. While underscoring the normative authority of the modern western nuclear family, the Indian family planning materials are careful not to refer to the extended family and not to question male authority in families. (Chatterjee and Riley, 2001:832)

In recent years, the issue of family planning has been broadened to make family welfare a people's movement; the approach is voluntary and educational.

Health Education

When India attained political freedom, the health services, particularly in rural areas, were rudimentary; life expectancy was under 30 years, the death rate as high as 50 per thousand and the infant mortality rate around 130 for every 1,000 births. There was little awareness among the public about health, hygiene, nutrition, and the media had to take the messages on such vital issues to the grassroots. Delhi Doordarshan introduced a weekly programme on health in the late 1960s and other *Kendras* also started telecasting similar programmes in due course. The programmes generally consisted of either an interview with a medical professional on a particular disease or a discussion on one of the latest developments in the area of medical research. Sometimes the viewers were invited to send questions about their medical problems and, depending on the type of questions received, a specialist in that field was invited to answer them.

The programmes did help in increasing awareness about the causes of many diseases and their treatment. But one reason why they were criticised was because they covered diseases affecting only a small section of the public while ignoring vital public health issues. Similar criticisms have been voiced about medical research also, but the priorities for the television programmes were determined by the producers who might not be aware of the importance of providing public health programmes relevant to the masses. It is also possible that breakthrough in areas like heart transplants, cancer cure and so on had more glamour value than the on-going schemes on malaria eradication, tuberculosis detection and similar preventive and socially relevant public health schemes.

A case in point is the government attempt to track the progress of AIDS/HIV epidemic in the country. The government agrees that AIDS cases are grossly under reported (India, 2003:224) and has established a National AIDS Control Programme to fight the epidemic and to increase its awareness in the communities. The potential of the entertainment-education approach in the fight against the AIDS epidemic is explored by Singhal and Rogers (2002). In their most recent study,

Singhal and Rogers (forthcoming) discuss *Jasoos Vijay* (Detective Vijay), a collection of ten detective case stories, broadcast on Doordarshan 'to raise awareness about HIV/AIDS, shift social norms about the disease, and to reduce stigma'. Broadcast for ten months from June 2002 to April 2003, *Jasoos Vijay* is part of 'an intensive HIV/AIDS media initiative involving the Indian government's National AIDS Control Organisation (NACO), *Prasar Bharati* (the Indian national broadcaster), and the BBC World Service Trust (BBC WST). This India HIV/AIDS initiative is the largest media initiative ever funded by the British government's Department of International Development (DFID) (Personal communication from Professor Singhal).

Fitness programmes

Health programmes generally dealt with diseases and their treatment – the curative aspects were generally emphasised – but when Doordarshan started its early morning transmissions in 1987 they introduce a new genre of programmes on fitness and exercises. These programmes were targeted at younger audiences and became quite popular. Yoga as a way of controlling body and mind also had much coverage on Doordarshan and this in turn created, at least in urban areas, a high level of awareness about the need for regular exercise. Early morning walkers and joggers became a common sight in many cities.

Immunisation programmes

One of the notable successes of the media in public health has been in the area of immunisation of children against various killer diseases. Though Maternal Health and Child Care (MCH) has always been a part of the public health programmes even in the early years of independence, immunisation did not have the priority it deserved. MCH remained a separate area, not integrated with other public health and family welfare programmes. It was later realised that the survival of children was an essential prerequisite for the acceptance of permanent family planning methods and immunisation was accorded a national priority.

All the available media were utilised to spread the message of the importance of immunisation and Doordarshan launched a series of educative programmes, including short films on immunisation at prime time. Popular personalities, film stars, sports celebrities endorsed the message and the country achieved, and in some cases exceeded, the high targets fixed for immunisation.

Applied nutrition

Concomitantly, many programmes on Doordarshan dealt with nutritional values of locally available food varieties and the televised demonstration of cooking and serving helped in the acceptance of these items in homes. Applied nutrition items were woven into the regular programmes meant for women and for audiences in rural areas.

Women in televised Indian soap operas

Doordarshan *Kendra* Delhi started a programme for women in the late sixties. This weekly programme was patterned on similar lines to those popularised on radio – a composite programme of three or four items, with a narrator providing the link. The topics covered included health, grooming, childcare, leisure time activities, festivals, anniversaries, cooking and so on. The programme also provided a forum for projecting the artistic talents of women in groups. Talks, interviews, discussions, demonstrations, dramatic presentations were the general formats used, with occasional documentaries and docu-dramas.

Many social issues, from dowry to adoption of family planning, were taken up in the programmes, but politics was generally avoided and the whole approach was towards maintaining the status quo, praising the traditional norms and beliefs.

In traditional Indian society, there were definite and consensual norms of behaviour that regulated the conduct of women – all of them handed down from the past. For example, the concept of woman as *Sita* is prevalent in Indian society. Sita, immortalised in *The Ramayana* and portrayed in the epic soap opera, is the ideal woman, the ideal wife; she is steadfastly loyal to her husband and obeys his wishes unquestioningly. *The Ramayana* says that a wife's god is her husband: he is her friend, her teacher. Her life is of less consequence than her husband's happiness.

All these views are consistent with the traditional view of the woman as a source of power and the nation as Mother Goddess and with *Manusmriti*. This law of Manu has had a profound effect in shaping the morals of Indian society. Women's roles were essentially as mother (Ma), wife (Patni) daughter (Beti) and daughter-in-law (Bahu). A female should be subjected in childhood to her father, in youth to her husband and when her husband is dead, to her children. A woman must make every effort to honour the memory of her dead husband.

Do these norms find articulation in the Indian soap operas on Doordarshan and ZeeTV? There is no doubt that discourses of feminism are threaded around, on the one hand, 'discourses of traditional femininity and, on the other, liberating feminist discourse' (see Munshi 1998:574 for a useful discussion). However, generally speaking, soap operas telecast on Doordarshan in the 1980s tend to emphasise the traditional role of women while those on ZeeTV favour the liberated westernised woman. This is consistent with our findings in the majority of the soap operas telecast on Doordarshan and in *Amanat* and *Aashirwaad* telecast on ZeeTV (see particularly the observations/comments made by respondents of *Amanat* and *Aashirwaad* noted in Chapter 4).

In Doordarshan's *Hum Log*, women were portrayed in their traditional roles: home-bound individuals who derive their meaning in life through their husbands and children. Women were shown in passive, subordinate roles and were defined only in relation to men. In their study, Malhotra and Rogers (2000) found that western influences in India in the 1990s have resulted in changing notions of the 'ideal' woman. They found that women were becoming more visible in television programming but their roles were still constructed through '...patriarchal and nationalist interests often reverting any progress made in gender role portrayals to a more traditional status quo' (p 407).

Mankekar made similar observations about *Hum Log*

> Ironically, although one of *Hum Log's* purported objectives was to bring about a change in the status of women, its most important women characters are all depicted unsympathetically. The grandmother, Dadi, contrasts with Dadaji (the grandfather): where he is wise and selfless, she is vain, greedy and lacks 'common sense'. More important, while Dadaji often takes up the cause of his granddaughters and daughter-in-law, Dadi is insensitive to their suffering... (1999:110)

In the 1980s there was a series of soap operas on Doordarshan which discussed women and the family: *Buniyaad, Rajani, Humraahi, Udaan I & II*. Mrinal Pande, a journalist complained that

> the break-up of patrilineal family structure and the rise of the nuclear family has constantly been presented (through films and popular literature) as the symbolic beginning of some horrifying future, which will destroy morality ... which will masculinize the females by allowing them the choice of an identity and, horror of horrors, extend to them the freedom to exercise that choice... (quoted in Mankekar, 1999:112)

The image of the new Indian woman on satellite channels is of someone who exercises choice.

Women are portrayed as liberated, career-conscious and independent. The images are openly sexual too. Apart from issues of abortion, treatment of sexuality is quite candid. According to Page and Crawley

> Vidhynt Bhagwant, Director of the Women's Studies Centre in Pune, believes that the new channels are definitely opening up doors of sexuality. She sees a growing consciousness of the body and greater concern with one's looks. She says: 'Now, a fully body-conscious Indian woman is definitely not unreal... Even in the serials, the middle-aged woman is shown fit, dancing, singing ... and this is not only an upper class phenomenon... There is a definite zeal about looks and the outer form... (2001:168)

However, this preoccupation with looks and form has led to reported cases of anorexia and bulimia, especially among the urban affluent class, and a sharp increase in plastic surgery for enlarged or smaller breasts, fat removal, and nose re-shaping (Chopra and Baria, 1996 quoted in Singhal and Rogers, 2001:125). Clearly western television influences in India are changing the image of the ideal Indian woman, formerly portrayed with 'large breasts, substantial thighs and an abundant stomach' (Malhotra and Rogers, 2000:411).

The construction of this new image of the Indian woman is echoed in advertising. She is targeted by the advertising industry, which is careful to depict a modern liberated woman, emancipated but non-western. Following Munshi's (1998) arguments and taking into account globalisation and market forces, the emergence of this new Indian woman is now explored in terms of the traditional categories of mother, wife, daughter and daughter-in-law.

The mother

While motherhood remains the strongest component for advertisers – urging mothers to buy what is good for the family – mothers now fulfil a variety of roles. They are no longer just homebound; they are co-breadwinners and family makers. Consequently, changing circumstances call for changing modes of discourse. It is no longer necessary for mothers to spend much time preparing food: the scientific angle of the advertisements for food products provides reassuring statements about the needs of a healthy family. Thus

> the soft drink concentrate company Rasna ad pictures smiling children with their mother who declares 'when my children drink Rasna V, I feel better too. The nutritional chart pictured alongside detailing how the various 'vitamins Niacin and folic acid' help with 'good vision, healthy skin ... release of energy ... growth ... healthy blood and body tissues' leaves the consumer in no doubt. (Munshi, 1998:579)

Furthermore, to suit the Indian palate, Basmati flakes are available – 'toasted, not fried, and 98 per cent to 99 per cent fat free and 100 per cent cholesterol free'. As Munshi (1998:580) argues, the new mother is now a friend to her children, relying on Maggi Noodles to feed her young children happily when they return home from play. Indeed, the commercial success of Maggi Noodles can be gauged by the fact that their sales rose from none in 1982 to 1600 tons in 1983, 4200 tons in 1985, 10000 tons in 1990 and 15000 tons in 1998. More significant, the success of Maggi Noodles made packaged foods not just acceptable but, because of their convenience and modern image, desirable to the middle classes.

The wife

Many images of Indian wives on soap operas televised on ZeeTV picture them as rather independent human beings, able to make decisions on their own. Thus *Sailaab* (The Flood) telecast on ZeeTV in 1997 addressed the issue of 'what if an ex-love comes back into your life after you are married and have the responsibility of a family?' The dutiful housewife, Shivani, decides to stay with her husband. Advertisements reinforce this new situation in the relationships between couples. The advertisement for Onida washing machines shows a wife buying the machine with the help of her children and presents it as a *fait accompli* to her husband (Munshi 1998: 581). The ad for Horlicks shows the housewife holding up a jar proclaiming 'He may be a doctor. But when it comes to the family's health I decide what everyone eats...' The Anne French hair remover cream wife is portrayed as having gone from, 'don't you want his approval' to 'I feel soft and silky and woman all over'

The daughter

If there is some ambivalence in the attitude of wives towards their husbands and children – Shivani in *Sailaab* also took into consideration the welfare of her children before making up her mind to stay with her husband – daughters have far more freedom than before. In *Hum Paanch* (We Five) telecast in 1997 on ZeeTV, the story revolves around a middle class family with five daughters. The parents are in traditional roles – the father works and provides for the family while the mother is a housewife. The father's first wife is deceased, but at particularly interesting or difficult moments in the serial, the photograph of the dead wife comes to life, putting the father in his place and commenting on what's happening in the family. Among the five daughters, Radhika works outside the home, Sweetie is an aspiring beauty queen and Kajol Dada is a tomboy who abhors anything feminine and also refers to herself in the *masculine gender* (our emphasis).

The daughter-in-law

The new status of the daughter-in-law is sharply observed by Munshi (1998:581). A decade ago, television commercials for Sanifresh depicted

> ...the daughter-in-law holding her breath in terrified fear while her mother-in-law checked every corner of the house for any offending dirt. Military music playing in the background clearly underscored the mother-in-law's superior hierarchical position. Today, the popular Ariel commercial has the daughter-in-law politely but firmly converting her mother-in-law to the whitening powers of Ariel as opposed to older detergent powders. (1998:582)

The kind of self-assurance that many daughters-in-law have acquired vis a vis their traditionally dreaded mothers-in-law has been underlined by advertising companies such as *Trikaya Grey* whose executive Vice President is reported to have said that

> Research and consumer tracking profiles clearly indicate that today's women like to see themselves and others more in control than in earlier times. (Munshi: 1998:582)

The surveys and workshops undertaken by the Media Advocacy Group and published in May 1997 (personal communication from B. S. Chandrasekhar, formerly Director of Audience Research Unit – *Prasar Bharati)* are informative. The group assessed viewers' responses to the depiction of women on television and analysed some of the major concerns of the viewers.

The participants were divided into three categories: students, homemakers and working women. Within each group there were subgroups and various categories of girls and women, representing a whole range of viewers. The cities chosen were Delhi, Lucknow and Ahmedabad. The aim of the Media Advocacy Group was to help a cross section of society, particularly the less privileged and the less visible, to interpret media imagery and to provide them with a platform to collectively assert their reservations and problems with the media (p2).

The categories covered in the analysis by the Media Advocacy Group included depiction of

- the bold woman
- working women
- women as homemakers
- sexual harassment
- pregnancy and the single woman
- rape
- marriage

Some of the effects of soap operas identified by the Media Advocacy Group include the following:

- Soap operas have provided role models ranging over a wide gamut. The positive role models of bold women who are courageous enough to fight for their rights have given strength to some women.

- Soap operas portray an assortment of women in diverse circumstances. They range from the sacrificial prototype of Indian womanhood to independent, bold, assertive and often villainous women flaunting their sexuality. This has helped to broaden the horizons of women.

- There is a general feeling among young women that they can be polite, soft and feminine, but feel they should be strong enough not to give in and should fight for their rights.

- There is also a feeling that soap operas are not projecting an accurate image of working women. Working women are generally depicted as home-breakers, divorcees who seek numerous sexual relationships.

- There is greater assertiveness in choosing the spouse and the soap operas have brought home the message that the marital relationship is contractual in nature and requires active efforts from both the man and the woman to maintain a marriage.

- Soap operas have also dealt with widowhood and the sexuality of the widow.

- Soap operas have been able to help promoting better understanding of the sexual harassment of women and the need to provide protection from such harassment. The soap operas have also shown diverse options for a single woman who becomes pregnant.

- Rape has also been treated in sensitive ways, bringing out the real trauma of women exposed to it.

- Women are realising that marriage is not an end in itself but a means of fulfilling or attaining a higher status in life. The soap operas also carry the message that getting married is no guarantee of a lifetime relationship. Post-marital problems including extra-marital relationships can follow.

It is clear both from the results of our case studies and the conclusions of the Media Advocacy Group that feminism as understood in the West has not succeeded in mobilising Indian women. As Menon has, in her study of Oriya Hindu family practices, pertinently pointed out

> feminism as an intellectual perspective and a movement, is located in a particular historic and sociocultural context, and therefore, has little relevance in contemporary India. (2000:97)

Indian women do not accept the ideology of individualism inherent in a feminist approach which seeks to dismantle their family structures and target their husbands as oppressors. Some twenty five years ago, Mitchell noted

> the self-contradictory ideology of the (modern) family; on the one hand, it strove to preserve the family as a unit, ascribing to the mother and wife the central responsibility for the task; on the other it constantly encouraged the 'increasingly disruptive individualism' of its members. (1977:156ff)

This attack on Indian traditions has been voiced by India's ruling Hindu nationalists who argue that

> the growing presence of foreign satellite television networks undermines Indian traditions and promotes Western-style decadence. (Sharma 1998:13 quoted in Chadha and Kavoori 2000:426)

One of the ways in which this is happening is that in the competition between satellite channels and Doordarshan for revenues audiences are being viewed and targeted as consumers rather than as citizens. This is explored in the next chapter.

CHAPTER 7

The public service ethos and the ideology of consumption

The binary opposition set up by the distinction between consumers and citizens arises from the notion that while Doordarshan upholds the nation state and the fostering of citizenship values through its public service, the satellite channels have wholly different objectives. Through their transnational commercial flows of culture and information, they are deemed to challenge the sovereignty of the nation-state by consuming entertainment and trivia, creating globalised and hybridised identities (McMillin, 2002:127).

Doordarshan and the Public Service ethos

The idea of Public Service Broadcasting (PBS) is rooted in the notion of the enlightenment of the audience and a public space in which social and political life unfolds democratically (Chandrasekhar, 1999). PBS is also generally expected to create a sense of national identity among its audience and encourage excellence in programming. The early history of Doordarshan reflects the concern of the Indian government to aid in economic and social development in order to forge a nation out of the enormous diversity of political, religious, geographical and linguistic entities that composed independent India. In sharp contrast to commercial broadcasting which tries to cater to the needs of consumers, PBS addresses the citizens of the country and is concerned about issues affecting them. While the popularity of programming and the dependence of its sponsorship on audience ratings are paramount to commercial channels, the needs of the audience are what matters in PBS. Some of the other salient features of PBS are:

- universal accessibility
- universal appeal
- particular attention to minority tastes
- distance from vested interests
- guidelines that liberate rather than restrict programme makers

Doordarshan worked directly under the government and thus could not claim to be free of vested interests. Doordarshan did provide a public space for discussions on social and economic issues, but this was until recently virtually closed to political debates. A study conducted by the Media Advocacy Group (Shivdas, 1994) on women and men in the News found that during the period of study 'hard news' accounted for 59% of total news items. Events and people connected with politics dominated the hard news. As expected, men had an overwhelming presence – 298 (86%) men featured against 56 (14%) women. Across the board, men in the news were shown in diverse roles but women were either in the top echelons of the government or wives of dignitaries or sportspersons.

In the Regional News in Kannada, of the 206 personalities featured during the same period, 178 (86.5%) were men and only 28 (13.5%) women. In Marathi News from Mumbai, of the 299 stories covered, women were centre-stage in six of the 299 stories covered and only 2% of coverage gave them prominence. Women represented 3.5% of the total number of persons presented in the news during the study. As part of its public service ethos, Doordarshan has contributed significantly to improving the awareness of people on various issues especially in the following fields:

- literacy and education/ educational programmes
- agriculture and rural development
- public health, hygiene and family planning
- empowerment of women and other gender issues
- environment and ecology
- popularisation of science.

Most of these issues have already been discussed. There remains the role of Doordarshan in education and in science and environment programmes.

Educational programmes

Educational Television (ETV) programmes were introduced in India on October22, 1961 when Delhi Doordarshan beamed programmes to 250 schools provided with television sets.

The programmes were syllabus-oriented with the initial objective of improving the standards of science teaching at middle and secondary school levels. Three programmes, each of 20 minutes duration, were telecast five days a week. Each targeted the students of a particular standard or year. Television viewing was integrated with classroom teaching – a forty five minute period was divided into three: five minutes for preparing for the subject of the day, twenty minutes viewing time and twenty minutes of discussion led by the classroom teacher. The final evaluation of this experimental service showed that television did produce some positive results. The level of learning significantly improved and the television screen, even though only black and white, was more effective pictorially than a text-book.

When the experiment was extended to other centres, school television programmes were introduced. In Mumbai and Chennai they were syllabus-based programmes, whereas Srinagar *Kendra* decided to have 'general enrichment programmes' for its school children.

The success of ETV largely depends on the cooperation of the state educational authorities and teachers in schools. In Delhi, for example, the timings of the telecast were decided in consultation with the educational authorities, but in other places this was not always possible. There were other problems too. What language should be used as a medium of education has been a contentious issue. The state governments were keen on using the language of the state, but certain sections of the population preferred English. More students opted for the English medium in urban schools although in rural schools the regional language was generally the only medium available to students. Television adopted the regional language as the medium. Consequently, urban students benefited far more than their rural counterparts, particularly as the reach of signals was limited – the signals could reach only a few villages. Gradually ETV was given a low priority in the programmes of a *Kendra*, both for economic reasons and because more transmission time was devoted to entertainment. By the year 2000 just two *Kendras* were producing ETV programmes and interest in them dwindled.

Higher Education programmes

In collaboration with Doordarshan, the University Grants Commission (UGC), the authority in charge of higher education in India, started its Country-Wide Class-room (CWC) in August 1984. The CWC programmes were all in English and the UGC had set up production facilities at three levels: the Mass Communication Research Centre (MCRC), the Education Media Research Centre (EMRC) and the Audio Visual Research Centres (AVRC).

The CWC covers all subjects included in the University Curricula such as social sciences, pure and applied sciences, languages and literature, history and geography. According to Doordarshan (1996), the objectives of these programmes are:

- to put quality education within the reach of the students in small villages and towns

- to iron out the disparities caused by lack of facilities, good teachers and other amenities in many colleges in the country

- to acquaint teachers and students with the latest developments in different disciplines.

A survey conducted in 1993 by ADMAR (unpublished report), a private marketing research agency, estimated that about 19 million viewers were watching the UGC programmes at that time. The viewers consisted of both the target audience i.e. those taking part in undergraduate courses and also a non-target audience, i.e those who were not studying but enjoyed educational programmes.

The extent of viewership varied from region to region, with the east, south and north east higher than central and west India.

A similar study conducted in 1997 (unpublished) estimated that the total reach of these programmes had increased in four years to 22 million viewers. In 1997 DD-1 was reaching about 300 million and 22 million viewers of UGC programmes formed only 7% of the total audience. An increase of 3 million viewers in four years during which the television reach had almost doubled may not sound all that encouraging, but it should be remembered that viewers had many alternatives.

Science and Environment

In the early years of planning, attention was concentrated on the rapid development of heavy industry and large irrigation dams and environmental issues were neglected. The rapid depletion of forest cover, the alarming rise in the pollution level of rivers, the mushrooming of slums in cities witnessed in the 1950s and 1960s brought environmental issues to centre stage. On the basis that insufficient attention was being paid to ecological subjects in the media, Doordarshan was asked to educate viewers on various issues connected with the preservation of the environment and the maintenance of an ecological balance.

Jawaharlal Nehru wanted the highest priority to be given to popularising science so that people would be able to overcome superstition and blind beliefs. Consequently, Doordarshan *Kendras* have special chunks of science programmes where the progress in science, its application to day-to-day affairs, and the achievements of Indian scientists are brought to the viewers. Two series on the national network, *The Quest* and *The Turning Point,* deserve special mention. *The Quest* was produced in house at Calcutta. It dealt with everyday phenomena and its aim was to encourage a spirit of enquiry. *The Turning Point* was a science magazine, telecast between 1991 and 1995. It started as a monthly programme, then went fortnightly and finally weekly. Its aim was to demystify science and make people appreciate that science was not just about laboratories. *The Turning Point* was immensely popular and one particular episode generated more than 11,000 letters asking for information, making suggestions for future programmes and pointing out inaccuracies.

With broadcasting until recently a monopoly of the government, it has consistently maintained that the state-controlled Doordarshan is acting as a public service, even though government has been run at different times by political parties of opposing ideologies.

When India embarked on massive development and social change through its Five Year Plans, the public service function of broadcasting was redefined to include popularisation of the Plan schemes. Separate units were set up in all major stations to highlight the objectives of the Five Year Plans and the achievements made through them. These Plans emphasise issues such as raising agricultural production, improving the status of public health, and involving women in a larger way in nation-building activities.

Until the 1960s the ruling Indian National Congress had massive support from elected representatives, both in the federal Parliament and in most of the state legislatures. By the middle of the 1970s however, opposition to the central leadership was building up and the ruling party wanted to use radio and television to counter political opposition and project its leader as the champion of the downtrodden engaged in eradicating poverty and fighting the forces that exploit the poor.

These shifts in emphasis were reflected more in the information programmes of the media, particularly the news bulletins, and there was little change in the format and content of educational programmes. The only entertainment on television which had mass appeal was the weekly feature film. Doordarshan produced some other entertainment programmes in drama and music, but these were usually highbrow: classical and semi-classical music or adaptation of literary works.

By the early 1990s a combination of factors led to a dramatic transformation of broadcasting policies. One can trace some of these factors back to the 1970s when advertisements began, to 1980 when colour television was introduced, to the effects of the 1982 Asiad Games, to the commercial sponsorship of television programming on Doordarshan in the 1980s and to an emerging middle class. The policies of liberalisation initiated by Indira Gandhi in 1980, extended by her son Rajiv, and accelerated by the sweeping measures of economic reform implemented by the government of Narasimha Rao in the early 1990s created the conditions for the opening of a vast new market and a hitherto untapped demand for consumer products (Page and Crawley 2001:112). But it was above all the challenges posed by satellite channels in the 1990s that account for this dramatic transformation.

As we have seen, Doordarshan tried to fight off the satellite channels in a number of ways. These included

- increasingly using private programme production in the 1980s
- increasingly depending on advertising revenues to fund state broadcasting
- expanding the broadcasting distribution infrastructure through state investment in the 1980s

• liberalising electronics import policies

'The choices and developments expanded the public and private infrastructure for the consumption of media services without increasing public programme production capabilities' (McDowell, 1997:154). Nevertheless, many viewers turned to the satellite channels because they felt that Doordarshan marginalized their voices and was obsessed with a Hindu-centric view of India. Many felt that Doordarshan's public service broadcasting ethos was exclusionary. Consequently, the consumption of commercial media fare was, according to McMillin (2002), an act of resistance against Doordarshan which, it is widely believed, promotes a North Indian Hindu supremacy and a Hindu state.

The satellite channels are credited with catering to people of all classes, but mainly to the emerging middle classes in India. Who are they?

The Indian middle classes

There have been studies of the Indian middle classes (Dubey, 1992; Varma, 1998) as well as surveys such as that of the National Council of Applied Economic Research (NCAER, 1998). Both Mankekar (1999) and Page and Crawley (2001) have addressed this issue and, drawing on all these sources, we can say that, according to some estimates,

• the Indian middle classes are variously estimated to number between 100-200 million depending on how they are identified.

• these new middle classes consist of professionals, salaried employees of state bureaucracies, small-scale entrepreneurs, traders, and prosperous farmers, and represented households earning annual incomes between $400 and $1,867 (Mankekar 1999:75)

However, Page and Crawley (2001:111), quoting NCAER survey of 1998, identify three distinct classes by their patterns of consumption rather than their income:

• the very rich category – 1 million households – six million people with an annual income of Rs215, 000 or more at 1993-94 prices (i.e. about $ 600 p.m). The top range of this middle class included a few hundred thousand who were wealthy even by international standards. But it was overwhelmingly the middle class of a poor country

• a further 'consuming class' of 150 million people – 30 million households – had an income level of Rs 45,000 to Rs215000 per annum (above US $90 per month)

• a third category – 50 million households – 275 million people – had an income level of Rs 22000 to Rs 45000 per annum (above US $44 per month)

Page and Crawley (2001) label this last category 'social climbers' and identify another category – aspirants – 50 million households or 275 million people – with an income level of Rs 16000 to Rs 22000 per annum (above US $22 per month).

This typology categorises the people of India with consumer power – over half the population. Also in this typology is the membership of today's middle classes associated with new lifestyles and ownership of certain economic assets. What is interesting here is that the categories of the new middle classes are open to members of different castes. A survey conducted by the Centre for the Study of Developing Societies, Delhi in June-July 1996 and reported in de Souza revealed the following features:

> ...the middle class, which at the time of Independence almost inclusively consisted of English – educated members of the upper castes, expanded to include the upwardly mobile dominant castes of rich farmers during the initial three decades after independence. In other words, this period saw the emergence of a small rural-based middle class. It is interesting to note that the criteria used to categorise this middle class was self-identity. Thus, from among those with middle class self-identification, respondents possessing two of the following four characteristics were included in the category 'middle class'
>
> 1. ten years or more of schooling
>
> 2. ownership of at least three assets out of four – motor vehicle, TV, electric pump set and non-agricultural land
>
> 3. residence in a pukka house – built of brick and cement and
>
> 4. a white-collar job. (2000: 259)

However, whatever the criteria, the advertising industry has had a field day since the 1990s. So while advertising expenditure as a percentage of gross national product in India '...was still well below global averages at the end of the 1980s, expenditure on advertising had grown from Rs2.5 billion in 1980 to Rs 7.5 billion in 1986 to a level of Rs 10 billion in 1990' (McDowell 1997:160). ($1 equivalent to 26 rupees in 1992-1993.) And 'this expansion is reflected in the growth of computers, two wheelers, cars, travel and tourism, hotels, office equipment, electronics, consumer durables and (processed) food' (McDowell 1997:160).

As we have seen, it is mainly women whom the advertising industry targets. There is comparatively little academic research on the effects of advertising on children. One of the few fruitful studies of the impact of advertising on children is that by Unnikrishnan and Bajpai published in 1996.

Children, Advertising and Consumerism

Predictably, Unnikrishnan and Bajpai (1996) found that advertising did have an ideological function since it seeks to create an environment conducive to manufacturers and marketers.

What are some of the dominant images that child-specific advertising in India promotes? The consumption of sweets follows a general pattern – chocolates are Dairy Milk and Cadbury, although children from wealthy families prefer (imported) Swiss chocolates. And the following table reveals to some extent the impact of drinks advertising.

Favourite Cold Drink Ads by Class
(In order of preference)

Upper Class	Middle Class	Lower Class
1. Pepsi	Pepsi	Rasna
2. 7 Up	7 Up	Pepsi
3. Thums	Up Citra	Maaza
4. Citra	Thums Up	Rooh Afzah
5. Miranda/Maaza	Maaza	Zeera Sip/7 Up

(Unnikrishnan and Bajpai, 1996: 261)

Clearly,

> brand images and class choices go hand-in-hand. Up-market commercials such as Pepsi and 7 Up have won favour with children from upper and middle class homes: the media hype that went with the launch of these products was not lost on people with the big bucks! (Unnikrishnan and Bajpai, 1996:265)

The top favourite advertisements chosen by the children in the same study include Ariel (detergent), Pepsi, Ever Ready (batteries) British Airways and 7 Up. Predictably, girls showed more interest than boys in personal care products. However, unlike the situation in the west, children watch a lot of TV with their parents, and the advertising industry is sensitive to this.

There is scarcely any sociological work on the impact of advertising on men. And yet the rapid growth of advertising and marketing in India and the policies of economic liberalisation described here have made their presence strongly felt in mainstream India, reflecting the consumer culture in urban Indian lifestyles. This is evident not only among the middle classes in India, with their designer clothes and accessories, but more importantly among the general members of the public. Those who can afford it, like the rickshaw-pullers, sport their designer sunglasses and clone their appearance on screen icons.

Adapting Jameson's (1991) remarks about the impact of postmodernism in the social sciences, it can be said that the impact of advertising in the soap operas on satellite channels such as ZeeTV has brought about:

- a whole new culture of the image
- a whole new technology
- a whole new utopian realm of the senses.

The net effect of this impact is in many ways similar to the adoption of advertising imagery in films like *Maine Pyar Kija* (I Have Fallen in Love, 1989):

> rich, saturated colour effects constantly emphasising surface,
> trendy costumes (the cooks wear red-check coats), green
> fields full of footballs... ice falling into glasses of Coke, a
> heroine with fluffy top and a leather-jacketed hero who
> loves motor-bikes, posters of American pop icons...
> (Rajadhyaksha and Willemen, 1994:451)

All these images are contextualised in an Indian ambience, just as they are in Indian popular cinema. The advertising industry has indianised its content and its imagery to suit the Indian viewers.

CHAPTER 8
Indian soaps and society

This exploratory journey into the world of televised Indian soap operas has revealed their role and impact on Indian audiences. The unique textual form that these soap operas exhibit affords valuable insights. But this study also reveals some of the difficulties presented by televised soap operas to this social scientist interested in their impact on Indian society.

Consequently, this concluding chapter evaluates the connections the book has made between Indian soap operas and the way Indian society is evolving. It begins by looking back at Doordarshan's contributions through its soap operas to national integration, identity and citizenship in India and then moves to the soap operas on the satellite channels in the light of a globalised India. Underpinning the discussion is an assessment of theoretical and methodological frameworks used so far and the book ends with a consideration of televised Indian soap operas of the future.

National integration, identity and citizenship in India
There is no doubt that the fundamental changes worldwide and in India in particular can be largely attributed to technology and the information industry. Until the arrival of satellite channels in the 1990s, Doordarshan was committed to its stated mission of public service and enjoyed, especially in the 1980s, an unprecedented boom in its transmission capabilities, its television coverage and its advertising revenues. With soap operas such as *Hum Log, Humraahi* and others based on the Education-Entertainment Communication Strategy, Doordarshan achieved some success in mobilising opinions regarding birth control, welfare issues and the empowerment of women. In their comprehensive analysis of *Hum Log*, Singhal and Rogers (1999) demonstrated the benefits to the audience/viewers that this soap opera has conferred. What concerns us here is the issue of identity. In the doctoral dissertation of Malwade-Rangarajan (1992, quoted in Singhal and Rogers, 1999:73-74), *Hum Log* is shown as adopting a two-fold strategy to structure the national consciousness of its viewers. An Indian identity was depicted as being in opposition

to a Western identity, and Indian identity was defined in terms of the coexistence of multiple regional identities. Thus, according to Malwade-Rangarajan, episode 16 of *Hum Log* depicted certain practices which were considered Indian. For example, touching one's parents' feet or asking for their blessings was definitely Indian whereas kissing people on the cheek or cutting a cake was decidedly un-Indian.

Episode 18 showed how the various religious subgroups in India could coexist. Issues of caste were raised, but the main point was that the caste system should be downplayed. Being a Hindu is compatible with respecting people of other religious backgrounds.

Testing how audiences from different linguistic and socio-economic groups in Delhi interpreted *Hum Log's* preferred readings of national identity, Malwade-Rangarajan found that most rejected the Indian v/s Western dichotomy. They believed that an Indian identity was made up of 'certain Western customs and modes of behaviour on the one hand, and regional customs and modes of behaviour on the other' (from the abstract to Malwade-Rangarajan's doctoral dissertation) This would not be inconsistent with the views of the middle classes. Malwade-Rangarajan's study of identity formation demonstrates that audiences play an active and sophisticated role in the process of communication.

The preferred reading of the telecast versions of the *Ramayan* and the *Mahabharat* is equally clear. Deliberately or not, these two epic soap operas were instrumental in providing a Hindu-centric vision of India and they affected issues of national integration and identity. How then did the public service ethos of Doordarshan, as expressed in the soap operas discussed in this book, help towards a revisioning of the Indian nation and the uplift of its citizens?

It is pertinent to compare Doordarshan's public service ethos with that of the BBC. According to the British government, broadcasting is a public utility and the BBC was mandated to develop a national service in the public interest. The interpretation of this public service ethos was left to the broadcasters and, above all, to Lord Reith, the first Director General of the BBC from 1927 to 1938. Lord Reith saw the BBC as emblematic of national culture and his vision for it was encapsulated by his famous phrase that broadcasting exists to educate, entertain and inform.

The chief executives of Doordarshan followed the three Reithian objectives, projecting the broadcasting medium as an instrument of national development. Echoing Lord Reith's strategy, they sought to maintain high standards for its programmes. In the process, they sidelined entertainment.

Here the comparison falters. Many Indians cannot afford to pay any licence fee and the considerable class and regional variations which exist in India are ill served by Doordarshan. Consequently, the values of equal citizenship are not properly realised within a democratic country. There is an obvious dissonance between the legalistic rights of all citizens enshrined in the Indian Constitution and the brutal realities of the day to day lives of at least half of India's population. There are unequal relationships among cultural/religious and social groups in India. To take language as one example: although Article 29 (1) of the Constitution states that 'Any section of the citizens residing in the territory of India or any part thereof having a distinct language, script or culture of its own shall have the right, to conserve the same' (Quoted in Mohapatra 2002:174), language is clearly one area of inequality. Mohapatra notes that

> language is fundamentally social and a right to preserve one's own language is inescapably a collective right. This, the Supreme Court declared, includes even the citizens' right to agitate for its protection. (2002:174)

Mohapatra further quotes Article 30(1) of the Constitution of India which states that

> the State shall not, in granting aid to educational institutions, discriminate against any educational institution on the ground that it is under the management of a minority, whether based on religion, or language. (2002:174-175)

Language choice is one aspect of identity; religion is another. However, the right of minorities to have their own educational institutions and the distinctive identities of the linguistic and religious minorities of India give rise to a tension between the majority and the minority populations and have serious implications for equal citizenship. At least two examples spring to mind regarding this tension and its implications for equal citizenship values:

- the granting of special rights and privileges to the Dalits, the scheduled tribes and the OBCs. The recommendations of the Mandal Commission (1990) meant that these three low caste groups, making up over half the population, would have at least 50 per cent of central Government positions set aside for them.

The government's policy is a balancing act – in Weiner's (2001:200) words: 'a commitment to equal rights for all (article 15) with special benefit to some' (article 15(4).

- the tension inherent in such a policy is clear. Weiner defines the tension as being between 'on the one hand, the goal of a casteless society in which the individual is the unit of public policy and, on the other, the concept of reservations for scheduled castes and tribes with the group as the unit of public policy.'

Who is actually an Indian is problematic. Indians have cross-cutting multiple identities For example, are Muslims in India Indian Muslims or Muslim Indians or Muslims *tout court*?

Oomen points out that an overwhelming number of Muslims and Christians are converts from the Dalits and the Scheduled Tribes, and argue that if one takes...

> the criterion of nativeness seriously, a majority of both the Muslims and the Christians have a better claim to be Indian nationals because the Aryan Hindus, who claim to be the original inhabitants came to India only some 3,500 years ago. (1997:84)

Yet there is tension and friction in the relationship between the Hindu majority and the Muslim minorities, who are often seen as the enemy within.

According to Shariff,

> 43 per cent of Muslims (and 27 per cent of Christians) live below the poverty line in comparison to 39 per cent of Hindus. Here too there are considerable regional variations within India – for example, compared to other states, more of the Muslim population in Uttar Pradesh and Bihar are poor. (1999:44)

The demand for special privileges by Muslims, highlighted in recent years by the Shah Bano controversy (see note at the end of this chapter) has brought into question India's commitment to secularism as an ideology of the State ever since independence. In a letter to the Nawab of Bhopal written on 8 July 1948, Nehru said

> I believe in India being a secular state with complete freedom for religious cultures and for co-operation between them. I believe that India can only become great if she preserves that composite culture which she had developed through the ages. I confess however that doubts sometimes assail me whether this is going to happen or not... (quoted by Mohapatra, 2002:176)

The demolition of the *Babri* Mosque in December 1992 confirmed Nehru's doubts and marked a turning point in the history of secularism in India. There is no doubt that the telecasting of *Ramayan* and *Mahabharat* in the 1980s contributed significantly to this historical turning point.

It is fruitful to reflect briefly on this phenomenon since the last two decades have seen the rise of belligerent ideologies of intolerance leading to 'toxic communalism', as Praful Bidwai put it at a conference at the School of Oriental and African Studies (London) in 2003. By becoming one of the biggest importers of armaments and by accelerating the nuclearisation of India, the BJP and its associates have effectively obliterated the fourth Nehruvian principle, non-alignment, mentioned in our introduction. Doordarshan has certainly projected a Hindu-centric view of India. This is consistent with the explicit mission of the BJP and its associates to 'get even' with history and to develop a particular notion of Indianness and, more importantly, a particular notion of the Hindu. The soap operas, by contrast, include all communities. Like the Indian popular cinema where icons such as Nargis (Mother India), Dilip Kumar, Shabana Azmi, Salman Khan, Amir Khan, Shah Rukh Khan and many lyricists, music composers and producers are Muslims whose contributions to the pleasures of Indians are inestimable, the soap operas demonstrate the kind of harmony in which various communities and castes can live side by side as do, for example, *Chacha* Ahmed and Lala Lahori Ram in the soap opera *Amanat*.

The coming of satellite channels on the 1990s and the economic liberalisation policies that began in the 1980s propelled India into the twenty-first century in yet another way. The satellite channels (ZeeTV, Sony, StarTV among others) demonstrate beyond doubt a kaleidoscope of western culture and promote consumerism – a trend in which consumer lifestyles and mass consumption influence taste and fashion. The consumerist world view promoted by a global culture is gaining ground in India, as elsewhere. In the words of Sklair

> The technical revolution in telecommunications and information systems has made possible the worldwide spread of the 'culture ideology' of consumerism that transforms all the public mass media and their contents into opportunities to sell ideas, values, products...(1991:76)

Nearly half of India's population are now customers of this global culture which, in essence, remains bound to and dependent on western technology and the concentration of capital. In this, the role of the satellite channels is crucial. For while Doordarshan with its public service ethos views its audience as citizens to be educated, informed and entertained, the satellite channels construct their viewers as customers, to be entertained and to deliver products according to advertising requirements.

Until recently, the contrast between the soap operas telecast on Doordarshan and those on the satellite channels such as ZeeTV, Star and Sony was quite clear. Doordarshan's soap operas tackle issues concerning population and family planning (*Hum Log*), women-oriented issues (*Hum Log, Humraahi*), the soap operas telecast on the commercial satellite channels deal with the representation of the new Indian woman (*Tara*) and with having a good time. Doordarshan's unpopularity is due more to the way it tackled issues and the arrogance it displayed rather than to the intrinsic merit of the issues themselves. However, a factor consistently working against family planning as promoted in *Hum Log* is the joint family, a basic traditional unit in most of India today. In an uncertain world, an extended family provides a great measure of security, particularly when members of the family are old and dependent. Hence, the concept of a smaller family – a nuclear family – has little appeal. Furthermore a larger family represents power and when Hindus are told that Muslims and Christians do not restrict family size, there is real worry for the majority of Hindus lest they lose their numerical strength (see Nandy and Ramaprasad 1995:114-115; Rajagopal, 2001:302).

Another issue which causes grave concern is that of access and accessibility. It is unacceptable for a country which boasts of being a major player in the globalised world of the twenty first century to deprive half its population of access to television channels. What is required is both structural and institutional transformation. The basic needs of all Indian citizens: clean water, safe hygienic conditions and electricity, have to be met before one can truly say that India is playing its full role in a globalised world.

But can television compensate for society? This book ends on this question. How much can television do?

The validity of the studies

First it is necessary to establish the validity of the studies on televised Indian soap operas. Ninan's (1995) study is a journalist's approach to the emergence of television in India. It was billed as the first comprehensive study of television in India. It displays some of the best aspects of journalism showing, in particular, how state television as well as the satellite revolution impacted on the attitudes and habits of an emergent country.

Mitra's (1993) study is more academic and more specific. Focusing on culture as a set of everyday practices 'that constitute the lived experiences of various groups of people', her study examines the impact of the telecasting of the epic soap opera – *Mahabharat* – on the lives of Indians.

Mankekar's (1999) ethnographic study is about women and television in contemporary India. Focusing on the representation of women in the programming of Doordarshan, Mankekar provides illuminating insights into the ways in which women are positioned as key players in upholding national and family traditions – the central role of the family in Indian culture. Nationhood is emphasised throughout her study. Hers is probably the only study to provide details of the variety of soap operas on Doordarshan and how some of them such as *Hum Log*, *Rajani*, project women as 'bearers' of culture.

Rajagopal's (2001) study focuses on political culture and particularly on the reception and influence of the television serialisation of the *Ramayan*. Theoretically informed and ethnographically grounded, it provides excellent materials and some convincing arguments about how television was exploited by Hindu nationalists for propaganda purposes and how the changing nature of the language of politics in India provides an understanding of the phenomenon of the rise of *Hindutva* in India (p.2).

How convincing are these studies in enlightening us on the role and impact of televised soap operas on Indian audiences?

In an introductory article to the special issue of *Communication Theory* on entertainment-education (May, 2002), Singhal and Rogers chart a five-pronged theoretical agenda for future research on entertainment-education. Essentially, the article suggests 'a move beyond the Banduras and Sabidos' (personal communication from Professor Singhal).

Drawing on the above-mentioned sources, both the theoretical framework and methodological issues can be evaluated. Singhal and Rogers (1999:148) identified the following key concepts in their research on entertainment-education:

a) The Social Modelling Theory, with the behaviour of positive and negative role models presented in media messages

b) Individuals' self-efficacy

c) Parasocial interaction

With regard to a) and b) the work of Bandura (1977, 1997) is crucial. According to Bandura, an individual learns behaviour changes by observing and imitating the overt behaviour of other individuals who serve as models (Singhal and Rogers 1999:148).

As far as b) is concerned, self-efficacy is an individual's perception of his or her capability to deal effectively with a situation, and a sense of perceived control over a situation. Consequently

an individual who perceives herself as efficacious is more likely to adopt a family planning method because she believes that she can control how many children she has during her life time. (Singhal and Rogers 1999:150 quoting Bandura 1977, 1997 and Rogers 1995)

With regard to c), Singhal and Rogers (1999: 88-90) have indicated a high degree of parasocial interaction between audience members and television role models. Although Singhal and Rogers (1999) have conducted their study of *Hum Log* with much rigour and sophisticated quantitative techniques, the picture we have is only partial. Likewise, Brown and Brown and Cody (1991) have used sophisticated techniques to evaluate both the direct and indirect effects of exposure to *Hum Log* on respondents' beliefs. Although they found some evidence of prosocial television programmes affecting the cognitions of television viewers, Brown in particular has stated that

exposure to *Hum Log* was positively associated with viewers' awareness of the programme's prosocial messages... Viewers who were more exposed to *Hum Log* were also more likely to believe in women's equality and women's freedom of choice, but not in family planning... (1990:113)

Thus, although *Hum Log* was a highly successful soap opera, its success, as we have seen, was achieved after the producers toned down the original main objective of the soap opera – to promote family planning.

Clearly, as Singhal and Rogers (1999) have demonstrated, social psychological per-spectives and their methodologies do provide insights into the effects of televised Indian soap operas on audiences. But they provide snapshots rather than a compre-hensive understanding of the relationship between the audience and television. By concentrating on overt behaviour change and creating favourable attitudes, Singhal and Rogers (2002) do acknowledge the limitations of such perspectives since there is an overwhelming focus on behaviour change at an individual level. As they them-selves observe, quoting McMichael (1995)

> metaphorically speaking, entertainment-education scholars should go beyond investigating the bobbing of individual corks on surface waters and focus on the stronger undercurrents that determine where cork clusters are deposited along a shoreline (p.127-128).

So does the use of ethnography in both Mankekar's (1999) and Rajagopal's (2001) studies provide deeper understandings of the role and impact of televised Indian soap operas on Indian audiences?

The use of ethnography for the study of soap operas has become popular since the 1980s and has led to the publication of a number of analyses of soap operas already referred to. Both theoretically and epistemologically, the ethnographic studies by Mankekar (1999) and Rajagopal (2001), for example, differ from those by Singhal and Rogers (1999) and Brown (1990). As a method of qualitative research, ethno-graphy has an established tradition in the social sciences. Whereas quantitative research provides a high level of measurement precision and statistical power, qualitative television research provides greater depth of information and under-standing and is sensitive to the viewing practices and the ways in which television is interwoven into the fabric of modern everyday life. But ethnographic studies are not without problems. As Lull (1988) argues:

> What is passing as ethnography in cultural studies fails to achieve the funda-mental requirements for data collection and reporting typical of most anthro-pological and sociological research... Ethnography has become an abused buzz-word in our field. (quoted in Simpson 2001:26)

Ang's (1991:35) criticisms are more telling:

> No representation of the TV audience (empirical or otherwise) gives us direct access to any actual audience; it only evokes 'fictive' pictures of audiences in the sense of fabricated or made up... The social world of actual audiences is therefore a fundamentally fluid, fuzzy, and elusive reality, whose description can never be contained and exhausted by any totalising, taxonomic definition of television audience. (quoted in Simpson 2001:27)

Thus, while Mankekar's (1999) study provides illuminating insights into women-oriented narratives and Rajagopal's (2001) into the startling success of the ideologies of *Hindutva* in the 1980s and 1990s, what is missing in both studies is the ethnography of production. We need a broader perspective that includes the need 'to examine how programming content and format are truly negotiated between producer and consumer' (McMillin 2001:51). Indeed, the dimensions of the communication process – production, distribution, reception, the role of the script-writer, and their interdependence need to be addressed.

But even that would not be enough in itself. Ways of knowing, what counts as evidence, whose experience most counts and the act of knowing itself are all problematic. This brings us back to the original question. What we know depends heavily upon the links between epistemology, methodology and method.

In a recent publication, Gray (2003:2-3) has fruitfully examined these links. Warning against those who claim that ethnographic methods are the ones that give access to some real truth and 'that empirical work is the only kind of investigation that is worth doing', Gray asks a fundamental question:

> Why does the academic community invest so much power in these intellectual practices often to the detriment of other accounts or versions of the world? (2003:4)

Why indeed? Gray's question echoes the wars between the different theoretical and methodological approaches, particularly the sterile debate between those who espouse quantitative methods and those who favour qualitative methods. Oakley has persuasively argued in favour of a social science that can

> ...play a role in promoting evidence-based public policy; but often it has not done so... The process of understanding the contribution which experimental methods can make to this endeavour has been interrupted by the unfortunate ideological and political history outlined in this book. Women and social scientists, as groups possessing lesser power than men and natural/medical scientists, have been particular opponents of this ideology, often for understandable reasons. But the confusion of experimental methods with 'bad' science has been part of the social construction of methodology as a gendered configuration. The paradigm war has set us against one another in ways that have been unproductive in answering some of the most urgent social questions facing us today. (2000: 323)

The main objective of using a Cultural Studies/Sociological approach in this study is to situate the role and impact of televised Indian soap operas within the wider context of the relationship between television and society. My study does not use the full range of the tools available for a Cultural Studies approach. For example, there is no analysis from a semiotic perspective so this book does not cover approaches to visual analysis. Consequently, the question of visual representation and the question of the hidden meanings of images have not been addressed. A visual analysis of the *Ramayan* would provide more insights into its powerful spectacular effect. In the words of Rajagopal the predominant mood of the serial (*Ramayan*) cannot be conveyed by a discussion of its component parts. Much of the message is wordless, felt rather than heard, and communicated in the expressions and gestures of the actors... (2001:109)

Indeed, when launching a major new journal in 2002 – *Visual Communication* – Silverman said 'Images are central to our world. Yet, visual data has been strangely neglected in communication studies and qualitative research' (on promotion flyer).

Equally, there is no discussion of such theoretical trends as structuralism, postcolonialism, cultural populism and postmodernism in the present study. Nevertheless, it provides insights into the following:

- the growth of Doordarshan, the advent of satellite channels and their impact on the Hindi-speaking audiences through the fulcrum of the televised Indian soap operas

- the unique genre of the Indian soap operas has been highlighted and case studies examined

- the role of the audiences, particularly a sample in Delhi and Mumbai, has been explored along the variables of gender, class, identity, citizenship and nation

- the concept of globalisation informs the study

I have tried to open up the debate on the value of televised Indian soap operas by drawing attention to their marginalisation of such issues as poverty, disability, widowhood, sati, the dowry system. There is, however, another serious point to consider about soap operas in general. There is a feeling among academics that the study of popular culture of which soap operas are probably their best representative is not a relevant subject for academic inquiry. But the dramatic rise of the academic study of Cultural Studies in such countries as Britain, the USA and Australia suggests that the academic study of Cultural Studies is now taken seriously. Nevertheless, some fundamental problems remain.

Cultural Studies is an interdisciplinary subject, drawing its strengths from a variety of theories and methods from the Humanities and the Social Sciences. Because it is difficult to define precisely what Cultural Studies is, it is seen by many of its critics as a shapeless and incoherent subject. There may be an element of truth in this, as with the notion of Popular Culture. There are various conceptual attempts to define Popular Culture, hence the possibility of 'a conceptual and theoretically informed definition receiving widespread agreement' (Strinati, 1995:xviii) is difficult to envisage.

There are also problems with the concept of globalisation. Bauman (1998) acknowledges that globalisation exacerbates social differentiation and inequality by fixing some people in space and by restricting their access to the globally circulating capital and culture that others enjoy (see Kalpagam 2002). Is there any hope for the marginalized sections of the Indian society identified in this study?

Globalisation in India does not mean that the country acts like a cultural sponge – here the role of local cultures and in particular that of the Indian popular cinema is crucial to our understanding of pre-televisual India. As Sklair (1991) has argued, local cultures not only reinterpret or mediate transnational messages to modify their meaning but may also counteract these messages with messages of their own.

One way to counteract the negative effects of globalisation is to privilege the 'local'. As Kalpagam put it

> the 'local' is here taken to be the experiential site of the majority. Despite the operation of global forces and despite the fact that the site of the local is rapidly changing, these local sites that are 'heterotopias' in Foucault's (1986: 198) sense i.e. concrete places that provide meanings, resources and grounds for practices remain significant for the majority in the globalised world ... (2002:7)

Appadurai too has argued that

> the poor and powerless can participate actively in shaping practices of imagination called for by globalisation, but that the 'task of producing locality... is increasingly a struggle in the wake of globalising forces. (1996:189)

And he suggests that people can recover agency through a process of indigenisation that was deployed in resisting colonialism (quoted in Kalpagam 2002:8). Similar useful insights are offered by Nandy (1983) in his consideration of the issue of resistance by Indians under British Colonialism, when he identifies a cognitive and an ethical strategy of the oppressed that transcends the system.

With the regular launching of new soap operas worldwide and the need to revive ratings as a result of competition among the channels, concern has been expressed about their content which, according to Branigan (2002:5), is leading to more dramatic and sensational storylines involving boat explosions and plane crashes as well as the usual plethora of unsavoury episodes of murder, suicide, euthanasia, incest, rape, abduction, drug addiction, paedophilia and deaths from mystery viruses.

Equally worrying, particularly in the context of family in India, is the recent criticism of some of the popular soap operas telecast on British television. Under the headline, 'TV soaps are not fit for family viewing', Conlan reported that the Broadcasting Standards Commission had launched an investigation into the increasingly violent scenes in such soaps as *Coronation Street* and *East Enders* (*Daily Mail*, 10 May 2002).

This concern is echoed by India's new Chairman of the Censor Board of Film Certi-fication, BJP MP Arvind Trivedi Lankesh (who played Ravana in the epic soap opera *Ramayan*), who firmly believes in upholding Indian culture in all its purity. (*The Times of India* Special Report 27/07/2002 p1).

One reason offered for this new situation is that

> Historically, soaps have always been character driven, but in the last few years there have been attempts to make them more plot driven. As soon as you go down that path you have to find another big event and another. It's interesting to see how they dig themselves out of that hole. (Branigan, 2002:5)

Televised Indian soap operas, particularly those telecast on the satellite channels, are unlikely to be exempt from some of the more salacious and sensational aspects of proliferating soap operas.

While it would be fruitless to try to halt the consumption of McDonalds, Coca Cola, jeans, American English and the various aspects of the western media, it is widely agreed in India that the internalisation of western cultural values should not be at the expense of traditional values, particularly of family life. Consequently, the case for grassroots involvement such as that advocated by Kalpagam (2002) should be applied at all levels. This, in combination with the views expressed by Appadurai (1996) and Nandy (1983), would offer some hope, for as Kalpagam pertinently observes

> apart from the materialism and consumerism that the West has come to signify, it also stands for breakdown of family relations, high divorce rates, lesbian and gay relationships, dating, public kissing, children talking sex, Valentine Day celebrations, skimpy clothes, show biz and models. This is in many ways a reverse orientalism that Edward Said has critically examined how the West represents the rest. (2002:2)

This is not to suggest that all Indian traditions and practices should be preserved. Under the title 'Delhi's rich adopt gender selection of the poor', *The Times* in the UK reports how 'a deep-rooted preference for male offspring is threatening the balance of the sexes' (27/11/2002).

The role and impact of televised Indian soap operas on Indian audiences will be more fully and meaningfully understood if the following principles are applied to its study:

*   Soap operas require analysis from an integrated perspective by which their pro-duction and consumption involving texts, images, consciousness and reflexivity are looked at interdependently.

*   While satellite channels will telecast soap operas to audiences conceived as customers, the role of public broadcasting services such as Doordarshan is to

represent the national interest and serve the communities they see as citizens. For this to happen, Doordarshan needs to be managed by media professionals rather than bureaucrats and, as Raboy (1997, 1998) has made abundantly clear in his writings on the topic of Public Broadcasting Service, we need a new public culture that is global in scope but locally experienced.

- Soap operas are primarily for entertainment and are meant for consumption. However, the role of entertainment requires more academic studies in order to situate and explain as precisely as possible the particular pleasures and pain any aspect, in this case television operas, offers. This is all the more important in the case of televised Indian soap operas since, compared to those in the West, they have a much shorter telecast life.

- Any investigation into the role and impact of soap operas should include the totality of television programmes during the period under investigation.

- Apart from providing daily and/or weekly schedules of television programmes during the period of investigation, the influence of other media such as the press/magazines/the popular cinema/books should be taken into account.

Although this pilot study obviously has shortcomings, it was worth doing because of the unique genre and the vast audience characterising televised Indian soap operas. Moreover, soap operas have a role and significance in the cultural life of Indians, although on selected audiences.

Do the issues raised and explored in the study have any resonance with the Indian diaspora?

In an influential issue of the journal *Ethnic and Racial Studies* (2000), contributors provide illuminating insights into cultural identity, citizenship and national integration – the theme of the final chapter of the present study – as experienced by the Indian diaspora in the UK and the USA. Whether the Indian diaspora consists of Hindu Punjabis, Gujaratis, Muslims or Christians, argue the editors of this special issue,

> ...a consideration of Hindu nationalism and its impact on the diaspora can highlight key problems within debates on migration, diaspora, ethic and religious identity, 'fundamentalism', nationalism, culture and race. (Bhatt and Mukta, 2000:48)

They further state that several contributors to the journal argue that 'diaspora Hindu nationalism has been important for the ideological and political shape of Hindu nationalism in India' (2000: 409). Accordingly, Mukta explores

> the manner in which a wide variety of Hindu organisations, sampradays (sects), religious leaders and the diaspora Gujarati vernacular press has

mobilized active support for UK and Indian Hindutva causes during the late 1980s and 1990s. (2000:435)

While some contributors to this issue of the journal focus on the links between *Hindutva* in India and *Hindutva* in the west, others raise issues of secularism, identity and citizenship. Raj, for example, provides an ethnographic examination into how the language used by some young British Hindu activists 'promotes a Hindu identity in Britain within the complex area of Hindu nationalism and the politics of communication in the diaspora' (2000:552).

Some contributors suggest that debates on secularism engaged in by such Indian writers as Madan (1987) and Nandy (1988) (already referred to) raise

> ...important questions about the formation of citizenship, nation, community, and gender (am I a woman first before being a 'tribal', a dalit or a Muslim?)... (2000:410)

The repercussions from telecasting the epic soap operas – the *Ramayan* and the *Mahabharat* – are being felt far beyond India. As a considerable number of diaspora Indians watch televised Indian soap operas (this merits a separate study), what Rajadhyaksha and Willemen observed about Indian popular cinema '...for millions of Indian overseas, a major part of India derives from its movies' (1994:10) can equally be applied to televised Indian soap operas.

One of the urgent problems facing India now is how to achieve intercommunal harmony. Televised Indian soap operas, like the Indian popular cinema, make no distinction between Hindus and other communities and provide the kind of civic platform needed for a healthy democracy. However, televised Indian soap operas cannot function in a vacuum. The role of the state and the media is a crucial part of filling this vacuum. It is the case that a number of fundamental issues in India have not been adequately addressed in televised Indian soap operas. But responsibly planned and commercially sponsored soap operas can certainly contribute towards the education and uplifting of most Indians, particularly those who live in rural areas. Furthermore, in addressing the role of soap operas situated between television and Indian society, I endorsed, though not uncritically, much of what Mal Young, Head of Drama series at the BBC has said:

> The modern, socially aware soaps... are more powerful than politics in influencing attitudes. Governments come and go, policies change... But soaps provide the constant in our lives. They set out to reflect society, but end up affecting, gently changing, the way we think about our lives, and those around us. (quoted in Stewart *et al* 2001:285)

Note: The Shah Bano controversy is a *cause celebre*. In 1985, Shah Bano, a seventy-year old Muslim woman from Indore, sued her affluent lawyer husband for alimony from the time that he abruptly divorced her in 1978. Political interference meant that the Supreme Court upheld a decision under Islamic law that the former husband was under no obligation to pay alimony to his divorced wife.

Bibliography

Abercrombie, N (1996) *Television and Society* Cambridge: Polity Press

Abercrombie, N and Longhurst, B (1998) *Audiences* London: Sage

Adorno, T W (1991) *The Culture Industry: Selected Essays in Mass Culture* ed by J.M.Bernstein London: Routledge

Alasuutari, P (ed) (1999) *Rethinking the Media Audience* London: Sage

Allen, R C (1985) *Speaking of Soap Operas* Chapel Hill, N.C. University of North Carolina Press

Anderson, B (1991) *Imagined Communities* London: Verso

Ang, I (1985) *Watching Dallas: Soap Opera and the Melodramatic Imagination* London: Methuen

Ang, I (1989) Beyond Self-Reflexivity *Journal of Communication Inquiry* 13(2) p.27-9

Ang, I and Stratton J (1996) Asianing Australia: notes towards a critical transnationalism in cultural studies *Cultural Studies* 10 (1) p16-36

Aappadurai, A (1996) *Modernity at Large: Cultural Dimensions of Globalisation* Minneapolis: University of Minnesota Press

Appadurai, A (1988) How to make a National Cuisine: Cookbooks in Contemporary India – *Comparative Studies in Society and History* 30(1) p.3-24

Arsenault, H (1999) Giving soap operas thanks. Internet site: http/about.com December 3

Bandura, A (1977) *Social Learning Theory* Englewood Cliffs, NJ: Prentice Hall

Bandura, A (1986) *Social foundations of thought and action. A social cognitive theory* Englewood Cliffs: NJ: Prentice Hall

Bandura, A (1997) *Self-efficacy: The exercise of control* New York: Freeman

Barker, C (2000) *Cultural Studies – Theory and Practice* London: Sage

Bauman, Z (1998) *Globalization: The Human Consequences* New York: Columbia University Press

Bentley, E (1967) *The life of drama* New York: Atheneum

Bercovitch, S (1975) *The Puritan Origins of the American Self* New Haven: Yale University Press

Berkowitz, L (1984) Some effects of thoughts on anti- and prosocial influence of media events: a cognitive neoassociation analysis *Psychological Bulletin* 95 (3) p 410-427

Bhatt, C and Mukta, P (eds) (2000) *Ethnic and Racial Studies* vol 23 no 3 May

Billig, M (1997) *Banal Nationalism* London: Sage

Bounds, P (1999) *Cultural Studies* Plymouth: Studymates

Branigan, T (2002) Street stars face axe in bid to revive ratings *The Guardian* 5 January p.5

Brown, M E (1994) *Soap Opera and Women's Talk: The Pleasure of Resistance* London: Sage

Brown, W J (1990) Prosocial Effects of Entertainment Television in India *Asian Journal of Communication* Vol.1, No.1 p.113-135

Brown, W J (1992) Socio-cultural influences of prodevelopment soap operas in the Third World *Journal of Popular Film and Television* Vol 19 No.4, Winter p.157-164

Brown,W J and Cody, M J (1991) Effects of prosocial television soap operas in promoting women's status *Human Communication Research* 18 (1) p114-142

Brown, W J, Singhal, A and Rogers, E M (1988) Pro development soap operas: A novel approach to development communication *Media Development* 4 p.43-47

Cantor, M and Pingree, S (1983) *The Soap Opera* London: Sage

Chadha, K and Kavoori, A (2000) Media Imperialism revisited: some findings from the Asian Case Media, *Culture and Society* Vol.22 p.415-432

Chakravarty, S S (1996) *National Identity in Indian Popular Cinema (1947-1987)* Delhi: Oxford University Press

Chandrasekhar, B S (1999) Changing Audience Preferences – an Indian experience Public Service Broadcasting in Asia Compiled by *AMIC* Singapore

Chatterjee, N and Riley N E (2001) Planning an Indian Modernity: The Gendered Politics of Fertility Control *Signs* Vol 26 No.3 p.811-845

Chatterjee, P (1993) *The Nation and its Fragments: Colonial and Postcolonial Histories* New Delhi: Oxford University Press

Chatterji, P C (1987) *Broadcasting in India* New Delhi: Sage

Chen, M A (ed) (1998) *Widows in India – Social Neglect and Public Action* New Delhi: Sage

Cixous, H with C Clement (1987) *The Newly Born Woman* Manchester: Manchester University Press

Colley, L (1992) *Britons: Forging the Nation 1707-1837* New Haven: Yale University Press

Conlan, T (2002) TV soaps are not fit for family viewing *Daily Mail* 10 May

Connor, W (1993) Beyond reason: the nature of the ethno-national bond *Ethnic and Racial Studies* 16, p.373-89

Crabtree, R D and Malhotra, S (2000) A Case Study of Commercial Television in India: Assessing the Organizational Mechanisms of Cultural Imperialism *Journal of Broadcasting and Electronic Media* Summer, p.364-385

de Souza, P R (ed) (2000) *Contemporary India – Transitions* New Delhi: Sage

Doordarshan (1992) Cable and Satellite Television Report of a survey conducted in ten cities *Audience Research Unit* New Delhi: Doordarshan

Doordarshan (1996, 1997, 1999, 2000) *Audience Research Unit* New Delhi: Doordarshan

Dubey, S (1992) The Middle Class, in L A Gordon and P Oldenberg (eds) *India Briefing* Boulder Co: Westview Press p.137-164

Eldridge, J, Kitzinger, J and Williams, K (1997) *The Mass Media and Power in Modern Britain* Oxford: Oxford University Press

Frankel, F, R Zoya Hasan (2000) *Transforming India: Social and Political Dynamics of Democracy* Oxford: Oxford University Press

Gassett, Ortega Y (1932) *The Revolt of the Masses* London: Allen and Unwin

Gauntlett, D (1998) Ten things wrong with the effects of tradition in R.Dickinson, R Harindranath and O.Linne (eds) *Approaches to Audiences* London: Arnold

Geraghty, C (1991) *Women and Soap Opera* Cambridge: Polity Press

Giddens, A (1990) *The Consequences of Modernity* Cambridge: Polity Press

Gill, S S (1988) Why Ramayan on Doordarshan? *Indian Express* 8 August

Gilligan, C (1982) *In a Different Voice: Psychological Theory and Women's Development* Cambridge MA: Harvard University Press

Gokulsing, K M and Dissanayake W (1998) *Indian Popular Cinema: a narrative of cultural change* Staffordshire: Trentham Books

Goodwin, A and Whannel, G (eds) (1990) *Understanding Television* London: Routledge

Gray, A (2003) *Research Practice for cultural studies* London: Sage

Grossberg, L (1988) Wandering Audiences, Nomadic Critics *Cultural Studies* 2 (3) p.377-91

Gupta, N (1998) *Switching Channels – Ideologies of Television in India* Delhi: Oxford University Press

Hall, S (1981) Cultural Studies: two paradigms in T. Bennett, G. Martin, C. Mercer and J. Woollacott (eds) *Culture, Ideology and Social Process* Milton Keynes: Open University Press

Hawley, J S (ed) (1994) *Sati: The Blessing and the Curse* Oxford: Oxford University Press

Hayward, S (1996) *Key Concepts in Cinema Studies* London: Routledge

Herman, E S and McChesney, R W (1997) *The Global Media* London: Cassell

Herzog, H (1944) What do we really know about Daytime Serial listeners? in Lazarsfeld P F and Stanton, F *Radio Research 1942-1943* New York: Duell, Sloan and Pearce

Hirst, P and Thompson G (1996) *Globalisation in Question* Cambridge: Polity Press

Hobson, D (1982) *Crossroads: The Drama of a Soap Opera* London: Methuen

India (2003) *A Reference Annual* Publications Division: Ministry of Information and Broadcasting Government of India

Jameson, F (1991) *Postmodernism, or The Cultural Logic of Late Capitalism* London: Verso

Johnson, K (2000) *Television and Social Change in Rural India* New Delhi: Sage

Joseph A and Sharma K (eds) (1994) *Whose News? The Media and Women's Issues* New Delhi: Sage

Jung, C G (1970) *Archetypes and the collective unconscious* Buenos Aires: Ed Paidos

Kalpagam, U (2002) Perspectives for a Grassroots Feminist Theory *Economic and Political Weekly* 23 November p 4686-4693

Katz, E and Wedell, G (1978) *Broadcasting in the Third World* Cambridge MA: Harvard University Press

Kaviraj, S (1994) Crisis of the Nation-state in India *Political Studies* X L11 p.115-129

Klapper, J (1960) *The Effects of Mass Communication* New York: Free Press

Kohli, A (1990) *Democracy and Discontent: India's Growing Crisis of Governability* Cambridge: Cambridge University Press

Kohli, A (ed) (2001) *The Success of India's Democracy* Cambridge: Cambridge University Press

Krishnaraj, M, R, Sudarshan and A, Shariff (1998) *Gender Population and Development* New Delhi: Oxford University Press

Krishnan, P and Dighe A (1990) *Affirmation and Denial: Construction of Femininity in Indian Television* New Delhi: Sage

Lal, D (2000) The Third World and Globalisation *Critical Review* 14 No.1 p.35-46

Larsen, R and Haller, Beth A (2002) Public Reception of Real Disability: Freaks *Journal of Popular Film and Television* Vol.29 No.4 Winter p.164-172

Lazarsfeld, P and Stanton, F (eds) (1944) *Radio Research 1942-1943* New York: Duell, Sloan and Pearce

Lee, C (1981) *Media Imperialism Reconsidered: the Homogenizing of Television* Beverley Hills, CA: Sage

Leavis, F R and Thompson, D (1977) *Culture and Environment* Westport, CT: Greenwood Press

Leibes, T and Katz E (1993) *The Export of Meaning – Cross Cultural Readings of Dallas* Cambridge: Polity Press

Lewis, J (1991) *The Ideological Octopus* London: Rutledge

Lewis J (2002) *Cultural Studies – The Basics* London: Sage

Livingstone, S (1990) *Making Sense of Television: The Psychology of Audience Interpretation* Oxford: Pergamon

Lull, J (1980) The Social Uses of Television *Human Communication Research* 6, p.198-209

Long, E (1991) Feminism and Cultural Studies in R. Avery and D. Eason (eds) *Critical Perspectives on Media and Society* p.114-25, New York: Guilford

Lutgendorf, P (1990) Ramayan The Video. *The Drama Review* 34 No.2 Summer p127-176

Lutgendorf, P (1995) 'All in the (Raghu) Family' A Video Epic in cultural context in Babb, L.A. and S.S Wadley (eds) *Media and the Transformation of Religion in South Asia.* Philadelphia: University of Pennsylvania Press

Luthra, H R (1986) *Indian Broadcasting* New Delhi: Publication Division Government of India

MacLean, P (1973) *A triune concept of the brain and behaviour* Toronto, Canada: University of Toronto Press

Madan, T N (1987) Secularism in its place *Journal of Asian Studies* 46 (4) p.747-59

Malhotra, S and Rogers E M (2000) Satellite Television and the New Indian Woman *Gazette* Vol.62 (5) p.407-429

Malwade-Rangarajan, A (1992) Television and social identity: Audience interpretations of '*Hum Log*' Unpublished doctoral dissertation, Pennsylvania State University School of Communications State College

Mankekar, P (1999) *Screening Culture, Viewing Politics* Durham: Duke University Press

Marshall, T.H (1950) *Citizenship and Social Class and other Essays* (Published in 1964 as Social Class, Citizenship and Social Development) Cambridge: Cambridge University of Cambridge Press

Matelski, M J (1999) *Soap Operas Worldwide* Jefferson, North Carolina: McFarland

Mattelart, A (1979) *Multinational Corporations and the Control of Culture* Brighton: Harvester

McDowell, S D (1997) Globalisation and policy choice: television and audio visual services policies in India *Media, Culture and Society* vol 19 p.151-172

McMillin, D C (2001) Localizing the global – Television and hybrid programming in India *International Journal of Cultural Studies* 4:1 p.45-68

McMillin, D C (2002) Choosing Commercial television identities in India: a reception analysis *Continuum Journal of Media and Cultural Studies* Vol.16 No.1 p.135-148

McQuail D, (1997) *Audience Analysis* London: Sage

McQuail, D (2000) (4th edition) *McQuail's Mass Communication Theory* London: Sage

Menon, U (2000) Does Feminism Have Universal Relevance? The Challenges Posed by Oriya Hindu Family Practices *Daedalus* 129 no 4 p.77-99

Menon, N (1998) State/Gender/Community – Citizenship in Contemporary India *Economic and Political Weekly* 34 (5) 31 January p PE3-PE10

Mitchell, J (1975) *Psychoanalysis and Feminism* Harmondsworth: Penguin

Mitra, A (1993) *Television and Popular Culture in India: A Study of the Mahabharat* New Delhi: Sage

Mitra A (1994) An Indian religious soap opera and the Hindu Image *Media Culture and Society* Vol.16 p.149-155

Modleski, T (1982) *Loving with a vengeance* London: Methuen

Mohapatra, B N (2002) Democratic Citizenship and minority rights: a view from India in Kinnvall, C and Jonsson, K (eds) *Globalization and Democratization in Asia* London: Routledge

Morley, D (1980) *The Nationwide Audience: Structure and Decoding* London: British Film Institute

Morley D (1989) Changing paradigms in audience studies in Seiter, E, Borchers, H, Kreutzner, G and Warth E M (eds) *Remote Control: Television, Audiences and Cultural Power* London: Routledge

Morley, D (1992) *Television Audience and Cultural Studies* London: Routledge

Mukta, P (2000) The public face of Hindu nationalism *Ethnic and Racial Studies* Vol 23 No 3 May 442-466

Munshi, S (1998) Wife/mother/daughter-in-law: multiple avatars of homemaker in 1990s Indian advertising *Media, Culture and Society* Vol.30 p.573-591

Mytton, G (1999) *Handbook on Radio and Television Audience Research* Paris: Unesco

Naipaul, V S (1992) *A Million Mutinies Now* New York: Viking

Nandy, A (1983) *The Intimate Enemy: Loss and Recovery of Self under Colonialism* Delhi: Oxford University Press

Nandy, A (1988) The politics of secularism and the recovery of religious tolerance *Alternatives* 13,2 p.177-94

Nandy, A (1997) *The Secret Politics of Our Desires* London: Zed Books

Nandy, B R and Ramaprasad, J (1995) Thematic coverage of population and family planning efforts of India in the New York Times *Gazette* 56 p.101-122

Nariman, H (1993) *Soap Operas for Social Change* Westport, CT: Praeger

National Council of Applied Economic Research (NCAER) (1998) *Indian Market Demographics* New Delhi *National Readership Survey* (2001) India

Nightingale, V (1996) *Studying Audiences: the shock of the real* London: Routledge

Ninan, S (1995) *Through the Magic Window* New Delhi: Penguin Books

Norton, J H K (2001) (Fifth Edition) *India and South Asia* Connecticut, USA: McGraw Hill/Dushkin Company

Oakley, A (2000) *Experiments in Knowing* Cambridge: Polity Press

O'Donnell, H (1992) *Good Times, Bad Times: Soap Operas and Society in Western Europe* London: Leicester University Press (A Cassell imprint)

Oltean, T (1993) Series and Seriality in Media Culture *European Journal of Communication* 8.(1)

Oomen, T K (1990) *State and Society in India: Studies in Nation Building* New Delhi: Sage

Oomen, T K (1997) *Citizenship, Nationality and Ethnicity* Cambridge: Polity Press

Owen, G (2001) TV soap operas ' do best job of education' *The Times* 30 August p2

Oza, R (2001) Showcasing India: Gender, Geography and Globalisation *Signs* Vol.26 No.4 p.1067-1095

Population Communications International (PCI) (1994) A Report on a series of three surveys in the Hindi-speaking region of India to test the effect of the television serial Humraahi as a vehicle of social change. April New York: United Nations (Unpublished)

Page D and Crawley, W (2001) *Satellites over South Asia* New Delhi: Sage

Pandian, M S S (1992) *The Image Trap: M.G.Ramchandran in Film and Politics* New Delhi: Sage

Parameswaran, R E (1997) Colonial Interventions and the Postcolonial Situation in India *Gazette* Vol.59 (1)21 p.21-41

Raboy, M (ed) (1996) *Public Broadcasting for the 21st Century* Academia Monograph 17, Luton: University of Luton Press

Raboy, M (1997) The World Situation of Public Broadcasting: Overview and Analysis p.19-36 in *Public Service Broadcasting: Cultural and Educational Dimensions* Paris: Unesco

Raboy, M (1998) Public Broadcasting and the Global Framework of Media Democratization *Gazette* Vol.60 (2) p.167-180

Radway, J (1984) *Reading the Romance: Women, Patriarchy, and Popular Literature* Chapel Hill: University of North Carolina Press

Radway, J A (1988) Reception Study: Ethnography and the Problem of Dispersed Audiences and Nomadic Subjects *Cultural Studies* 2 (3) p.359-76

Rajadhyaksha, A and Willemen P (1994) *Encyclopaedia of Indian Cinema* London: British Film Institute

Rajagopal, A (1999) Communities Imagined and Unimagined: Contemporary Indian Variations on the Public Sphere *Discourse* 21.2 Spring p 47-83

Rajagopal, A (2001) *Politics After Television Hindu Nationalism and the Reshaping of the Indian Public* Cambridge. Cambridge University Press

Report of the Working Group on Software for Doordarshan (1985) An Indian Personality for Television New Delhi: Ministry of Information and Broadcasting

Robertson, R (1992) *Globalisation, Social Theory and Global Culture* London: Sage

Rogers E and Singhal, A (2000) Entertainment Education in Asian Nations *Asian Pacific Media Educator Issue* No.9, July-Dec p.77-88

Ruddock, A (2001) *Understanding Audiences* London: Sage

Saksena, G (1996) *Television in India: Changes and Challenges* New Delhi: Vikas Publishing House

Schiller, H (1976) *Communication and Cultural Domination* White Plains, NY: Sharpe

Schlesinger, P (1991) *Media, State and Nations: Political Violence and Collective Identities* London: Sage

Schlesinger, P (1992) Public Service Broadcasting *AMIC* Singapore

Sekhar, K (1999) Emergence of Religious and Regional Language Programming in Indian TV *Media Asia* Vol.26 No.1 p.41-47

Sen, A (1993) Pluralism *Monsoon* Vol.20, no.3, p27-46

Shah, A (1997) *Hype, Hypocrisy and Television in Urban India* New Delhi: Vikas Publishing House

Shariff, A (1999) *India, Human Development Report* Delhi: Oxford University Press

Shivdas, A (ed) (1994) *Women and Men in News and Current Affairs* New Delhi: Media Advocacy Group

Shurmer-Smith, P (2000) *India Globalisation and After* London: Arnold

Simpson, P (2001) Audience in *Critical Dictionary of Film and Television Theory* ed by Pearson, R E and Simpson, P London: Routledge

Sinclair, J, J, Elizabeth and S. Cunningham (1996) *New Patterns in Global Television: Peripheral Vision* Oxford: Oxford University Press

Singh, S (1995) The Epic (on) Tube: Plumbing the Depths of History: A Paradigm for Viewing the TV serialisation of the Mahabharata *Quarterly Review of Film and Video* Vol 16 (1) p 77-101

Singhal, A and Obregon, R (1999) Social Uses of Commercial Soap Operas. A conversation with Miguel Sabido *Journal of Development Communication* Vol 10 (1) p 68-77

Singhal, A, Obregon, R and Rogers, E M (1994) Reconstructing the story of 'Simplemente Maria' the most popular telenovela in Latin America of all time *Gazette* 54 (1) p1-15

Singhal, A and Rogers, E M (1987) Television Soap Operas for Development in India – *Paper Presented at the International Communication Association Conference*

Singhal, A and Rogers, E M (1989) Pro-social television for development in India in R.E. Rice and C.Atkin (eds) *Public Communication Campaigns* Newbury Park, CA: Sage

Singhal, A and Rogers, E M (1999) *Entertainment – Education: A Communication Strategy for Social Change* Mahwah, New Jersey: Lawrence Erlbaum Associates

Singhal, A and Rogers, E M (2002a) A Theoretical Agenda for Entertainment-Education *Communication Theory* May p.117-135

Singhal, A, and Rogers, E M (2002b) *Communication strategies for the AIDS epidemic* Thousand Oaks, CA: Sage

Singhal, A, M Cody, E M Rogers and M Sabido (eds) (2003) *Entertainment-Education and Social Change: History, Research, and Practice*. Mahwah N J: Lawrence Erlbaum Associates

Sinha, N (1996) Television and National Politics in Raboy, M (ed) *Public Broadcasting for the 21st century* Academia Monograph 17 Luton: University of Luton Press

Sklair, L (1991) *Sociology of the Global System* London: Harvester Wheatsheaf

Smesler, N J (1994) *Sociology* Oxford: Blackwell Publishing

Smith, A D (1992) National identity and the idea of European Unity – *International Affairs* Vol.68 No.1 p.55-76

Smith, P (2001) *Cultural Theory: An Introduction* Oxford: Blackwell

Snyder, L L (1976) *Varieties of Nationalism: a comparative study* Hinsdale: The Dryden Press

Sonwalkar, P (2001) India: Makings of Little Cultural/Media Imperialism *Gazette* Vol 63(6) p.505-519

Spender, D (1985) *For the Record: The Meaning and Making of Feminist Knowledge* London: Women's Press

Srinivas, S V (2001) Researching Indian Audiences *Cultural Dynamics* 13 (1), p.117-123

Srinivasan, K (1995) *Regulating Reproduction in India's Population: Efforts, Results and Recommendations* New Delhi: Sage

Stewart C, Lavelle, M and Kowaltzke, A (2001) *Media and Meaning* London: BFI Publishing

Storey, D (1998) Popular Culture, discourse and development – Rethinking entertainment-education from a participatory perspective. In. Jacobson, T and J, Servaes (eds) *Theoretical approaches to participatory communication* (p.337-358) Cresskill, NJ: Hampton Press

Storey, J (1993) *An Introductory Guide to Cultural Theory and Popular Culture* New York: Harvester Wheatsheaf

Storey, J (ed) (1996) *What is Cultural Studies? A Reader* London: Arnold

Strinati, D (1995) *An introduction to theories of Popular Culture* London: Routledge

Tamir, Y (1995) The Enigma of Nationalism: Review Article *World Politics* 47, p.418-440

The Hindustan Times (1999) 10 Shows that gave TV its Talking Points, 26 December

Thomas, D (1982 *The Experience of Handicap* London: Methuen

Thomas, P N (1993) Information and Change in India – Cultural Politics in a Post Modern Era *Asian Journal of Communication* Vol 3 no 1 p 64-83

Thussu, D K (ed) (1998) *Electronic Empires: Global Media and Local Resistance* London: Arnold

Thussu, D K (2000) *International Communication* London: Arnold

Tomlinson, J (1991) *Cultural Imperialism: A critical introduction* Baltimore MD: John Hopkins University

Tomlinson, J (1999) *Globalisation and Culture* Cambridge: Polity Press

Tunstall, J (1977) *The Media are American: Anglo-American Media in the World* London: Constable

Turner, G (1996) *British Cultural Studies* London: Routledge

Unnikrishnan, N and Bajpai S (1996) *The Impact of Television Advertising on Children* New Delhi: Sage

Vanaik, A (2001) The New Indian Right *New Left Review* 9 May- June p 43-67

Varma, P K (1998) *The Great Indian Middle Class* New Delhi: Penguin

Varshney, A (1993) Contested Meanings: India's National Identity, Hindu Nationalism and the Politics of Anxiety *Daedalus* 3 Vol.122 p227-261

Weiner, M (2001) The struggle for equality: caste in Indian politics in Kohli, A (ed) *The success of India's Democracy* Cambridge: Cambridge University Press

Williams, R (1976) *Keywords: A Vocabulary of Culture and Society* London: Fontana

Winston, B (1986) Debate has not halted the flow of blood *The Listener* 23 January p.9-10

Appendix A

Degree of parasocial interaction indicated in letters from *Hum Log* viewers

Indicators of Parasocial Interaction	Percent of Letters That Indicate Parasocial Interaction (N=500)
1. Strong involvement with characters	93
2. Likes and respects Ashok Kumar's epilogues	83
3. Compares personal ideas with those of characters	65
4. Perceives a character as a down-to-earth, good person	43
5. Talks to favourite character while watching	39
6. Feels that Ashok Kumar helps them make various decisions and looks to him for guidance	39
7. Adjusts time schedule to watch, to have a regular relationship with a television character	30

Source Singhal (1990). From Singhal and Rogers (1999:90)

Appendix B

At one level, the story of *The Mahabharata* can be summarised very simplistically as follows:

The Simplified Narrative Structure of Mahabharat and its Transformations

The conflict between

Good: evil

Dharma: adharma

concretised into a family feud

Pandavas: Kurus

composed of

Yudhistir: Duryadhan

Bhim: the Hundred

Arjun: Brothers

Nakul

Shahadev

Wife – Draupadi

Mother – Kunti and

Madri

Father – Pandu

Supported by

Krishna: Shakuni

resolved in the battle

of

Kurukshetra

where

the

Pandavas prevail

Thus dharma prevails

(Source: Mitra 1993: 114)

Appendix C

The Ramayana

Although in discussing *The Ramayana* we are referring to a broad range of texts and performative traditions, the core elements of the story 'a la Valmiki' and as used by Ramanand Sagar, the producer of the epic soap opera Ramayan can be simplistically described as follows:

King Dasra of Ayodhya had four sons from three wives: Ram, Bharat, Lakshman and Shatrugna. On attaining adulthood, Ram, the eldest, was married and was expected to succeed his father to the throne. However, his stepmother, Kaikeyi, wanted her son Bharat to become king. Remembering that the king had once promised to grant her (his favourite wife) any two wishes she desired, she demanded that Ram be banished and Bharat be crowned.

Ram was banished for fourteen years and, accompanied by his wife Sita and his brother Lakshman, lived in the forest. They were very happy in their new environment and Ram and Lakshman managed to destroy the evil creatures (rakshasas). However, one day a raksha princess tried to seduce Ram but was wounded and driven away by Lakshman. She retured to her brother Ravan, the ruler of Lanka and told her brother about beautiful Sita.

Ravan devised a system to trap Sita and abducted her. With the help of Hanuman and his army of monkeys, Ram and Lakahman fought Ravan and succeeded in freeing Sita. They returned to Ayodhya where Ram was crowned king. A glorious period of peace and prosperity – Ram Rajya – The Golden Age – ensued. Rajagopal (2001: 328) reports that in the last book of the Valmiki's Ramayana, rumours about Sita's fidelity during her captivity in Lanka forced Ram to banish his wife to the forest. There, Sita raised twins, Lava and Kusha. Years later, Ram met them and accepted them as his sons. The twins were reunited with their father, but Sita decided to return to earth, where she was welcomed by the earth goddess.

Appendix D

The percentage distribution of households by socio-economic status in cities (National Readership Survey 1997).

	SEC A	SEC B	SEC C	SEC D	SEC E
Top 8 Cities	14.7	18.3	22.1	21.6	23.4
1 million +	12.7	18.5	20.2	23.1	25.4
0.5 – 1 million	12.8	19.1	22.0	20.8	25.3
0.1 – 0.5 million	11.5	18.3	20.2	22.6	27.4
Below 0.1 million	8.3	16.2	19.4	23.7	32.3

This table reveals the size of the affluent strata (SEC A) in the cities and the size of the so-called middle class (SEC B and SEC C). For the soap operas, these two groups were the primary targets.

Appendix E

Some Recent Popular Zee Serials
(Soaps, Sitcoms and Crime Thrillers)

Title	Day of Telecast	Time of Telecast*
India's Most Wanted	Tuesday	10.00 p.m.
Hasratein (Yearnings)	Tuesday	9.30 p.m.
Amanat (Sacred Trust)	Thursday	8.30 p.m.
Hud Kar Di (That's The Limit!)	Monday	9.00 p.m.
Raahein	Tuesday	9.30 p.m.
Hum Paanch (We Five)	Daily	1.30 p.m.
Shapath	Tuesday	9.00 p.m.
X Zone	Thursday	9.00 p.m.
Aashirvad (Blessing)	Friday	9.30 p.m.
Ashiqui (Love (r))	Monday	8.30 p.m.
Kahan Se Kahan Tak (From where to where)	Wednesday	9.00 p.m.
Jagran (The Vigil)	Sunday	7.00 p.m.
Do Aur Do Paanch (Two and Two make Five)	Wednesday	8.30 p.m.
Mano Ya Na Mano (Accept it or Leave it)	Friday	10.00 p.m.
Darpan (Mirror)	Friday	2.00 p.m.
Commando	Monday	9.30 p.m.
Adhikar	Tuesday	10.30 p.m.
Neeyat (Purpose)	Tuesday	8.30 p.m.
Jaan	Thursday	10.00 p.m.
Tere Mere Sapne (Our Dream)	Saturday	10.30 p.m.

(* Indian Standard Time)

Index